The Well-Mannered Dog

DOG CARE
Companions™

The Well–Mannered Dog

From Dealing with Cats to Staying in Hotels, a Total Guide to Good Manners

From the Editors of

part of the family™

Edited by Matthew Hoffman

Rodale Press, Inc.
Emmaus, Pennsylvania

Library of Congress Cataloging-in-Publication Data

The well-mannered dog : from dealing with cats to staying in hotels :
a total guide to good manners / from the editors of Pets, part of the
family ; edited by Matthew Hoffman.
p.   cm. — (Dog care companions)
Includes index.
ISBN 1–57954–115–1   hardcover
ISBN 1–57954–260–3   paperback
1. Dogs—Behavior. 2. Dogs—Training. I. Hoffman, Matthew.
II. Pets, part of the family. III. Series.
SF433.W45 1999
636.7'0887—dc21   99–39662

Distributed to the book trade by St. Martin's Press

    4   6   8   10   9   7   5   3   hardcover

    4   6   8   10   9   7   5   3   paperback

Visit us on the Web at www.petspartofthefamily.com, or call us toll-free at (800) 848-4735.

OUR PURPOSE

To explore, celebrate, and stand in awe
before the special relationship between us
and the animals who share our lives.

The Well-Mannered Dog

CONTRIBUTING WRITERS

Sheree Crute, Susan Easterly, Tony Farrell,
Susan McCullough, Christian Millman, Jana Murphy, Amy D. Shojai

RODALE BOOKS

Editor: Matthew Hoffman
Publisher: Neil Wertheimer
Editorial Director: Michael Ward
Research Manager: Ann Gossy Yermish
Copy Manager: Lisa D. Andruscavage
Copy Editor: Kathryn A. Cressman
Cover Designer and Design Coordinator: Joanna Reinhart
Associate Studio Manager: Thomas P. Aczel
Book Manufacturing Director: Helen Clogston
Manufacturing Manager: Mark Krahforst

WELDON OWEN PTY LTD

Chief Executive Officer: John Owen
President: Terry Newell
Publisher: Sheena Coupe
Associate Publisher: Lynn Humphries
Senior Editor: Janine Flew
Senior Designer: Kylie Mulquin
Designer: Jacqueline Richards
Illustrator: Chris Wilson/Merilake
Icons: Matt Graif, Chris Wilson/Merilake
Production Manager: Caroline Webber
Production Assistant: Kylie Lawson

Film separation by Colourscan Co. Pte. Ltd., Singapore

CONTENTS

PART ONE

GOOD DOGS DO BAD THINGS

PART TWO

THE CIVIL DOG

PART THREE

MANNERS AT HOME

PART FOUR

THE WELL-TRAVELED DOG

PART FIVE

MEETING THE NEIGHBORS

Introduction

Every winter, thousands of dogs representing more than 150 breeds arrive at Madison Square Garden in New York City for the annual Westminster Kennel Club dog show. This prestigious event admits only dogs who are champions of record—meaning they've blown away all the local, state, and regional competition. If dogs were allowed to get college degrees, these dogs would all have *bark*-alaureates.

I go to the Westminster dog show every year because I love watching these canine Einsteins at work. And yet, I can't help thinking that all of this precision training isn't very practical. Sure, it would be nice if our dogs obeyed the command "sit" perfectly and looked both ways before crossing the street. But most of us would rather our dogs did the things that really matter. Like greeting the mailman with a quiet woof instead of tearing at the door, or politely sniffing cats instead of chasing them.

Molly, my Labrador, is a case in point. She's mostly well-behaved, although she occasionally interprets "come" as "run the other way." As I've discovered, however, obedience isn't the same as good manners. For example, no matter where I take her for walks, she invariably does her business on someone else's lawn, as if her own yard just isn't good enough. At home, she's an incor-

rigible garbage thief. She steals whatever leftovers she can find, then gets sick on the carpet.

Molly doesn't need more training. She needs an etiquette coach.

That's exactly what *The Well-Mannered Dog* is. The only etiquette book for dogs, it tells exactly how to help them behave in real-life situations. Forget about perfect sitting or heeling like a pro. It tells how to stop dogs from dribbling their breakfasts on the floor. How to teach them to respect your personal space. Even how to go to bed when you tell them.

Dogs do need to know the basics, of course, and it's up to us to teach them. That's why we've included a ton of useful tips on providing discipline, the best and most effective commands, and handling a leash without getting tangled.

Dogs will always be dogs, of course. They're always doing things that come naturally to them but that people consider unmannerly or merely gross. Take chewing. You'll discover the real reasons that dogs put their teeth to work, and what you can do to make them stop. Or cat chasing. Appearances to the contrary, dogs and cats aren't natural enemies. Most cat chasing, in fact, is really a case of mistaken identity (cats resemble the small, furry prey that dogs used to eat). You'll learn a number of useful ways to help dogs and cats get along.

All dogs want to be polite—not because bad manners get them sent to bed without their suppers, but because they want to please the people in their lives. Here you'll find hundreds of ways to help them learn more quickly and to remember what they learned. When to say "yes" instead of "no." When to be firm and when to turn your back. The best times to practice manners and the best places. (One trainer recommends practicing in beer store parking lots on Saturday afternoons.)

To shine on the social scene, dogs need to know more than basic good manners. So we talked to Liz Palika of Oceanside, California, one of the country's best-known trainers and author of *All Dogs Need Some Training*. She gave us step-by-step plans for teaching dogs special skills, such as bringing your slippers, turning on light switches, and waving goodbye. The tricks look fancy, but they're easy to teach in just a few lessons.

Just as some dogs always seem to be on their best behavior, others do things that are truly, well, a little strange. Like Stormy, a Labrador retriever who doesn't drink his water, but plays with it. Maggie, who insists on depositing her 78 pounds on people's laps. Lady, who steals the children's toys from the toy box. You'll be amazed by their exploits—and by the creative solutions that helped them behave a little better.

Whether your dog is a social embarrassment, a domestic terror, or simply a little rough around the edges, it's easy to give him the social polish that he deserves. You'll both appreciate the difference.

Matthew Hoffman

Matthew Hoffman
Editor, *Pets: Part of the Family* books

PART ONE

GOOD DOGS
DO BAD THINGS

All dogs do things we wish they wouldn't. It's not that they're stubborn or willful—though sometimes they are—but that their ideas about manners are different from ours. We shake hands; they sniff. We sit on furniture; they sprawl all over it. But despite these and many other differences of opinion, dogs are always eager to please. This makes it easy to teach them what we want them to do.

CHAPTER ONE

WHY MANNERS MATTER

Dogs with good manners are welcome anywhere.
Whether or not they sit on command or bring in the newspaper,
proper doggy etiquette gets them the love and attention they deserve.

Chooch is the kind of dog that people dream about. A reddish-brown Chow Chow, he has an adorable face and a heart of gold. He valiantly protects his family by keeping watch over the front door, and he's patient enough to allow kids to use him as a pillow as well as a play toy. And on the rare occasions when his owners skip a walk or two, he carefully positions his 85-pound body over the cat's litter box and takes care of business.

This Samoyed always drops what he's doing and comes immediately when he's called. That's the essence of good manners.

Chooch's owner, Janis Aquirre of Milton, Massachusetts, appreciates this dainty touch, although she has no idea how he learned it. Cassie, the cat, is less impressed. She clearly believes that Chooch is the rudest thing she's ever seen—after all, it is *her* litter box. This just goes to show that a dog's well-mannered gestures can become another family member's problem.

What Are Good Manners?

Dogs are always doing things that people (and cats) don't understand because their cultural backgrounds are so different. This difference in perspective makes the business of defining good manners an inexact science, at best. "What we call a behavior problem is most often a problem for us, not for our dogs," says Karen L. Overall, V.M.D., Ph.D., a certified animal behaviorist and director of the behavior clinic at the University of Pennsylvania School of Veterinary Medicine in Philadelphia.

A dog who chews shoes, for example, is just doing what dogs do. He may be confused in his choice of objects, but he doesn't intend any harm. A tough Rottweiler who growls at strangers through the door probably isn't mean; he's only displaying the protective talents common to his breed. And a dog who acts as though the living room is his very own Indy 500 track is probably blowing off steam and doesn't mean to drive you crazy.

But regardless of their individual backgrounds, breeding, and personal concerns, all dogs should know a few mannerly basics, says Joanne Howl, D.V.M., a veterinarian in West River, Maryland. At a minimum, they need to know the following rules.

- They shouldn't destroy the furniture.
- They should do their business outside and not in the house.
- They should come whenever you call.
- They should always walk politely on the leash, without pulling.
- They should respect people enough not to get aggressive.

Everyone would probably add a few personal concerns to the list, Dr. Howl adds. If you live with other animals or walk your dog in public, for example, you certainly want him to be calm around dogs and cats. Other people want their dogs to stop barking on request. To resist jumping on people. To not give wet kisses to

BREED SPECIFIC

Dalmatians are mighty cute in the movies, but in real life they can be a handful because they have an inherited tendency to be nervous and somewhat unsociable. They're great dogs, but they do best with people who are knowledgeable about training and who have an abundance of patience.

people who don't appreciate them. Dogs are adaptable and eager to please, so they usually don't have too much trouble learning what they're supposed to do, says Dr. Howl.

Good for People, Good for Dogs

The benefits of dogs being well-mannered are pretty obvious from the human point of view. Dogs who behave well and respect the rules become much appreciated members of the family, and other people like them, too.

Dogs get similar benefits, says Dr. Howl. They are very social. They feel best when others are happy with them and when they know what they're supposed to do and how they're supposed to act. "Dogs feel insecure when there are no guidelines for their behavior," she says. "They need structure because they come from a culture, known as the pack, that has regulations and hierarchies like our own."

Dogs who stay home most of the time can get away with knowing just the rudiments of etiquette. But those who travel—on vacations, shopping trips, or nice long walks around the neighborhood—need to know a little more. The better they behave in public, the more opportunities they'll have to be with their owners—and for dogs, that's the greatest reward of all.

The Key to Good Manners

Whether or not you give your dog a formal education—by taking him to obedience school, for example—he should understand that he always needs to look to you for direction. The easiest way to teach him this is to control—and

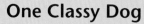

One Classy Dog

Greyhounds are known as intelligent, elegant dogs of superior breeding. Then there's Hattie. She has the intelligence all right, but her manners aren't exactly what you'd expect from a doggy debutante—especially one who lives with Karen L. Overall, V.M.D., Ph.D., a certified animal behaviorist and director of the behavior clinic at the University of Pennsylvania School of Veterinary Medicine in Philadelphia.

Hattie, who lives near a farm, loves nothing better than rolling in cow manure. Horse manure is good, too, but she prefers the bovine kind. And she really rubs it in, getting as much of the redolent stuff next to her skin as she possibly can. The smell can linger for days or weeks, until Dr. Overall can't take it anymore and gives her a bath. Hattie, of course, simply goes in search of more cow dung.

Experts have a lot of theories as to why dogs roll in dung, but Dr. Overall suspects that it's not very complicated. Hattie probably rolls in manure for the same reason that humans wear cologne. "She's just coating herself in her favorite scent and having a great time," she says.

let him know that you control— the one thing he loves best.

"Your dog has to understand that you hold the key to the food box," Dr. Howl says. Food is a powerful motivator, and dogs will do just about anything to get a little more. To clearly establish the link between food and manners, Dr. Howl recommends teaching dogs one simple rule: Nothing in life is free.

Before giving your dog food, have him do something for you. It doesn't matter what: sitting, lying down, coming to you, whatever. When he obeys—and when food is on the line, dogs are very cooperative—give him his meal.

He will have just learned an important rule: When he does what you ask, he gets fed. To really nail down this point, Dr. Howl recommends teaching it in all sorts of situations. Have your dog sit before you let him outside— and reward him when he does it. Practice a few obedience commands, and reward him when he gets them right. If you do this all the time, he'll always look to you for directions, and that's the secret to teaching good manners.

Dogs vary widely in their abilities, Dr. Overall says. Some learn quickly, while others need more time. Some dogs are stubborn and willful. Others are shy and high-strung. "People often choose dogs because they have certain ideas about breeds," she points out.

"That's not a good idea. All collies aren't Lassie, and all shepherds aren't Rin Tin Tin."

One way to establish leadership over your dog is to let him know that you control the food. This English springer spaniel knows that she must sit politely to earn her dinner.

CHAPTER TWO

THE MISCHIEF MAKER

Call it a culture collision. Even dogs with the best intentions will get into trouble because their idea of proper behavior is totally different from their owners'. Every breed—and every dog—has a slightly different agenda. Confusion and mischief are inevitable.

Shakti loves laundry, especially when it is fresh, neatly folded, and put away in a basket. When the moment is right, the 6-year-old Yorkie dives in headfirst and begins rooting around until she finds the prize—a tightly rolled pair of socks. Once she nabs the fuzzy toy, she embarks on a fun game of show-and-tell. She trots over to her owner, shows him the socks neatly clenched in her teeth, and then waits, her eyes glistening with anticipation. Her owner, predictably, leaps to his feet and lunges forward, trying to rescue the socks.

Not a chance. Shakti instantly takes off, with her sockless owner in hot pursuit. The game doesn't end until the socks have been retrieved or shredded beyond recognition.

Shakti is definitely a mischief maker, but not because she is bad or poorly trained. Quite the contrary. She is doing what her owner has inadvertently taught her to do, says Karen L. Overall, V.M.D., Ph.D., a certified animal behaviorist and director of the behavior clinic at the University of Pennsylvania School of Veterinary Medicine in Philadelphia. People chase dogs when they want to get things back. Dogs chase each other when they want to play. Shakti, interpreting her owner's behavior according to her rules, gleefully continues the game.

The Meaning of Mischief

Dogs certainly aren't saints. They do a lot of things that people wish they wouldn't. Stealing socks is hardly the worst offense. There are dogs who chew table legs. Who steal chicken bones from the trash and steaks from the counter. Who stand still as their owners approach with their leashes—then tear off with mischievous looks and amazing flurries of speed.

This mixed-breed puppy's idea of a good time is destroying rolls of toilet paper. His owner would certainly call it mischief.

One thing that dogs never do is cause trouble because of bad intentions. Most of the time, they're just doing things that dogs have always done. But that same behavior, put into a human environment, looks an awful lot like mischief.

"Most behaviors that we consider bad are just natural for most dogs," says Nicholas Dodman, professor of behavioral pharmacology and director of the Animal Behavior Clinic at Tufts University School of Veterinary Medicine in North Grafton, Massachusetts, and author of *Dogs Behaving Badly*. "Barking and digging up the yard certainly qualify. And any greyhound worth his salt, for example, will go after a rabbit."

Don't Blame Me, I'm Just a Puppy

If you ever get a chance to see dogs in the wild, you'll be amazed by the extent to which their doglike appearance belies their undoglike behavior. Dogs (and wolves) who have never been domesticated are suspicious, aloof, and fiercely independent. They don't crave affection from people. They don't need handouts. And they certainly don't listen to anything you have to say. They're opposite in every way from the dogs who share our lives.

For thousands of years, people have deliberately bred out of dogs their original independence and spirit, and bred in such traits as gentleness, soft features, and a desire to please. "Dogs have been selected for puppylike looks and behavior," says Joanne Howl, D.V.M., a veterinarian in West River, Maryland. "We like dogs who are perpetual puppies." With that

Most dogs have been bred to be puppylike into adulthood. A few, like basenjis, retain some of the independence of their wild forebears.

playfulness, however, comes a certain amount of youthful, immature behavior. Like it or not, we've essentially bred the little rascal into our dogs, Dr. Howl explains.

A few breeds have retained their original spirit, she adds. Basenjis, for example, which have become increasingly popular, are prized for their intelligence, gorgeous coats, and unusual voices. (They're known as barkless dogs because they make a curious yodeling sound.) Basenjis are wonderful dogs, but only if you're prepared to deal with their very strong independent streaks. They won't make a lot of mischief, because they aren't like puppies. But then, they probably won't be as affectionate as other dogs.

My Genes Made Me Do It

Every dog is an individual, but dogs also belong to breeds (or mixes of breeds), and breeds have different personalities—and get into different types of mischief, says Melissa R. Shyan, Ph.D., a certified applied animal behaviorist and associate professor of psychology at Butler University in Indianapolis. For example:

Australian shepherds. Bred to manage herds of sheep, these hard-working dogs have tremendous amounts of energy. This helps

them do their jobs in the fields, but at home in the living room, it puts them in a perpetual state of excitement. If they can't burn off their energy in an authorized fashion, they find other ways to do it, like zipping in circles around the couch for 10 minutes or herding wayward children and adults. And if they happen to topple a vase or two along the way, you can be sure it wasn't intentional.

Basset hounds. These warmhearted little hunting dogs are generally well-behaved, except for one thing: They love to bay, producing a mournful-sounding *arrrooowww*. It's not a bid for attention, just a throwback to their pasts, when they bayed to alert their humans that they'd cornered their prey.

Corgis. These dogs have received a lot of attention in the media because they're the dogs that Queen Elizabeth favors. For all their royal connections, however, these rough-and-tumble little dogs were bred to be hard workers. Owners sometimes complain that their corgis nip at their ankles or dodge between their feet when they walk—vestiges of their days as herders who had the job of rounding up livestock.

Irish setters. These happy, exuberant dogs can barely contain their enthusiasm for life. Along with their zest comes a certain amount of zany and impulsive behavior. But you have to consider their pasts. Generations of breeding have made them superb hunting dogs. An intriguing scent or a movement in the bushes is sure to arouse their curiosity and send them off in search of prey. This is considered talent when they're on the hunt. In the house or at the park, it looks like pure mischief.

Jack Russell terriers. Spunky, pint-sized, and full of energy, Jack Russell terriers can't depend on size to get what they want. What they do have is persistence, which they use to pester their owners into submission. They may lick hands until they get petted, for example, or jump up and tap their owners a few times—hard, when necessary—to get attention.

Labrador retrievers. No one is sure why they do it, but these sweet-natured dogs love to dig. They rarely bury things, but they turn yards into minefields of holes.

Lhasa apsos. These loyal, smart dogs are known for making a heck of a lot of noise when anyone or anything comes near the door of their abode. They originated in Tibet, where they were called *abso seng kye*, or "bark lion sentinel dog"— a very impressive name for a very small pup.

The mischief that dogs get into is partly determined by their breed. Corgis, bred to herd cattle, tend to nip at people's heels. Golden retrievers were bred to fetch game, so they like carrying things in their mouths.

Universal Mischief

A dog's breed is a big influence in his life, but it's not the only one or even the most important. Every dog, from the quietest springer spaniel to the rowdiest Labrador retriever, has to indulge his essential dogness from time to time. And dogs, regardless of their breeds, play by different rules than people.

Take chasing. Nearly all dogs do it, and they don't really care if the thing they're chasing is a tennis ball in the yard or a roll of toilet paper that they've knocked from its holder. Chewing, sniffing around for leftovers, and lifting their legs on vertical objects are just a few of the other ways that dogs express themselves. They can be taught not to do these things, but it's a challenge. These tendencies are just a part of who they are.

I Learned It from You

If you've ever wondered how smart dogs really are, try this experiment: Tip your plate one evening and let a scrap of steak slide to the floor. Your canine disposal unit will react to the arrival of this unexpected manna in two ways: First, he'll quickly grab the steak and scarf it down. Second, he'll return to the same spot just in case it happens again.

Dogs pay very close attention to the people in their lives. They try to understand what we're thinking and feeling, and to anticipate what we're going to do next. Even a dog who has never given a thought to human food can become a perpetual mooch if he tries it once and finds it good.

Some types of mischief, like mooching, may have their origins in things that occur accidentally. Many more occur because we inadvertently reward our dogs for the very things we'd like them to stop doing, says Dr. Shyan. Here are some examples.

Barking. Even small dogs can have very big voices, which is why barking is among the most common complaints that veterinarians—and neighbors—hear about. Barking is normal for dogs, but it drives people crazy. The usual response is to yell "Quiet!" But dogs don't understand that word. What they do understand is that you're barking along—and so they bark even louder.

Chasing. As Shakti the clothes hound can attest, nothing is more fun than running and

This Labrador mix loves to run and be chased. His owner may be desperate to get her laundry back, but to a dog, the chase is all a game.

Anything to Pass the Time

By the time he was 9 months old, Muttonhead had a very strong work ethic. One day when his family was gone, this industrious German shepherd decided to while away the time by doing a little housework.

He carried bedroom pillows downstairs and arranged them around the living room. He gently removed a set of delicate demitasse cups, one at a time, from the dining room sideboard and neatly lined them up on the couch. He finished his work by piling panty hose, socks, and other bits of clothing on the living room floor. On top of the pile went a single paperback book.

His owners were amused, but very surprised, by this strange behavior. So they talked to Melissa R. Shyan, Ph.D., a certified applied animal behaviorist and associate professor of psychology at Butler University in Indianapolis. It didn't take her long to figure out that Muttonhead had a surplus of energy and an uncommon amount of ingenuity. He was bored and needed something to do to occupy his time.

"As with many large young dogs who are left alone, Muttonhead found a few activities to entertain himself with," Dr. Shyan says. She recommended that Muttonhead's owners give him some fun toys to play with—preferably toys that required a little thinking on his part. This would keep his mind occupied and reduce his urges to redecorate.

tiny jaws around a size-10 sneaker. So we laugh. Now, flash-forward a year. Tiny puppy teeth have become adult molars and incisors, and discarded sneakers have been replaced with expensive Italian shoes. All of a sudden, it's not so cute. And the dogs can't figure out why they're getting yelled at.

No More Mischief

The great thing about dogs is how different they are from us. They're rarely serious and never grim. Their exuberance and puppylike behavior are the reasons we welcome them into our homes and hearts. A little mischief is a very small price to pay.

There's a difference, of course, between occasional misdeeds and serious misbehavior. Dogs who are destroying their owners' belongings aren't going to get a lot of love. Every dog needs to understand what is expected and what the rules are, says Dr. Overall. People, in turn, need to understand why their dogs do the things they do. It's the only way to help them behave a little better.

"You cannot completely eliminate an activity that's natural to a certain breed, but you may be able to reduce the intensity or frequency with which certain acts occur," says Dr. Shyan. Giving dogs toys they like, a lot of exercise, and a little bit of training and encouragement will keep most types of mischief in check. Your dog will still act silly, but he'll look to you for direction—and that's the biggest step of all.

being chased. Seems simple, but people have a hard time figuring this one out. When dogs don't come when their people tell them to or when they've picked up something that they shouldn't, their people take off after them—and dogs run away like it's all a game.

Chewing. Puppies love to chew, and people think it's pretty cute when they try to wrap their

STRANGE behavior

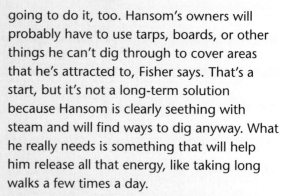

Name HANSOM

Breed JACK RUSSELL TERRIER

Age 2

The Behavior

Put Hansom on dirt, and he becomes a digging fiend. Once he gets going, the sky darkens with sprays of dirt thrown airborne by his whirring legs. For some reason, he does most of his digging at the fence. Some dogs tunnel in order to escape, but Hansom seems to do it just because he can. He chooses a spot, digs under the fence, then runs in and out through the hole, as though admiring his work. Over the years, the yard has taken on the appearance of a minefield; and flowers, plants, and grass rarely make it through the first season.

The Solution

Jack Russells are like merchant seamen: They just have to see what's over the horizon. Only instead of a boat, they have strong legs, tough paws, and inexhaustible amounts of energy. "This dog wants to see the world, and digging is one of the tools that Nature gave him to do it," says Betty Fisher, a trainer based in San Diego and co-author of *So Your Dog's Not Lassie*.

Dogs who dig digging won't give it up easily. Their ancestors did it, and they're going to do it, too. Hansom's owners will probably have to use tarps, boards, or other things he can't dig through to cover areas that he's attracted to, Fisher says. That's a start, but it's not a long-term solution because Hansom is clearly seething with steam and will find ways to dig anyway. What he really needs is something that will help him release all that energy, like taking long walks a few times a day.

Just chugging around the block won't keep this sailor in port, however. Calling Jack Russells "active" doesn't quite capture the type of seething energy that these dogs are born with. They need a *lot* of exercise.

Since Hansom craves a view of the world, Fisher recommends giving him one. A hole cut in the fence and covered with chicken wire would work. Better still would be to put the hole fairly high on the fence, with a small platform underneath. The platform doesn't have to be fancy, just some two-by-fours and a little plywood.

"Then he'd have a better vantage point than he could ever get from beneath the fence," Fisher says.

CHAPTER THREE

BEING THE DISCIPLINARIAN

Dogs crave direction in their lives. They used to get
this direction from other dogs. Today, they look to their
owners to tell them what to do and how to act.

No one wants to be the bad guy. You always feel that twinge of guilt whenever you push your dog out of your bed on a cold winter's night or tug the leash to the left when she so desperately wants to go right. Teaching obedience and giving reprimands are time-consuming and tiring, and they often seem to get in the way of dogs' good times. Who wants to tell man's best friend no?

Some people just aren't comfortable with wearing the sergeant's stripes. Dogs on the furniture? Nothing a vacuum cleaner can't take care of. Raiding the trash? Close the lid tighter and stash the can in the closet. Jumping on guests? Warn people ahead of time—and hope for the best.

The best never happens, of course. Unless dogs are shown what they should and shouldn't do, they're forced to make up rules as they go along, and their rules aren't going to be the same as yours. More important, dogs without discipline tend to be dogs without friends. When walking around the block is a perpetual tug-of-war, people are understandably reluctant to take the leash out of the closet. Dogs who jump on strangers don't get taken to public parks very much. And frenzies of barking can turn even the sweetest dogs into neighborhood pariahs.

Giving discipline isn't a lot of fun, but it pays off. Well-mannered dogs have advantages that their more unruly friends don't. These mixed-breed dogs know when they're allowed to play and when they should be quiet and out of the way. In return, they're allowed to spend more time indoors.

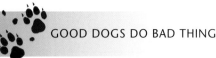
The Need for Leaders

Despite our natural reluctance to be taskmasters or scolds, dogs crave discipline. For 40 million years, they lived, played, hunted, and grew old within their family packs—carefully organized, close-knit groups of dogs who looked to their leaders, called alpha dogs, for instructions on how to behave and survive. Alpha dogs could be stern and demanding. But they always looked out for the welfare of the pack, and dogs understood and accepted this.

Good discipline is always friendly. Dogs form close bonds with people and want to please them. Most of the time, they need reminders more than reprimands.

Some dogs today have never seen a forest, much less lived in one, yet their need for leadership endures. Without other dogs to turn to, they look to us to take charge. Not because we're bigger or smarter, but because, just like the alpha dogs of old, we're the ones who control everything that they do. We control the food supply. We decide when they stay in and when they go out. We initiate play or insist on peace and quiet. In our dogs' eyes, we're very clearly the leaders of the pack, whether or not we take on the responsibilities that entails.

Being a leader involves more than giving orders and handing out discipline, says Suzanne Hetts, Ph.D., a certified applied animal behaviorist in Littleton, Colorado. Most of all, it requires giving clear directions about what is and isn't acceptable. Human society is incredibly confusing for dogs. They watch us closely for clues all the time. When someone comes to the door, for example, dogs aren't sure whether they're intruders or friends. Should they bark like crazy or wag their tails? They don't know unless their owners tell them.

"Dogs crave interaction, direction, and structure," says Ian Dunbar, Ph.D., a certified applied animal behaviorist in Berkeley, California. "They need rituals, and they like to know the status quo." In short, what they need most—indeed, what they crave—is guidance and a sense of what the rules are. They need discipline and won't be happy unless they get it.

Until fairly recently, most dogs got lots of discipline, mainly the wrong kind. Trainers and other animal experts (along with many human psychologists) believed that sparing the rod was spoiling the child. The goal of training was

Dogs don't regard discipline as cruel or unnatural. When dogs are together, older dogs will discipline the younger ones. Similarly, when dogs are with people, they expect to be told how to behave.

essentially to put dogs in their places, and some of the tactics used to achieve this could be very rough. Dogs certainly learned discipline. But they also learned to be afraid of punishment and even, in some cases, of their owners as well.

Teaching with Kindness

Most dog-training techniques originated with German or U.S. military trainers. Dogs essentially were treated as raw recruits who needed to be shouted down by tough drill sergeants or court-martialed into submission. Rather than getting praised for good behavior, they got a lot of criticism and punishment when they did something wrong.

Old-style training involved a lot of physical discipline. Trainers believed that humans should literally act like alpha dogs to enforce their rules.

CALL FOR HELP

Every person on Earth may belong to the same species, but our personalities are entirely different. You wouldn't expect the old man on the corner to act the same as the teenager next door, and even siblings are often so different that it's hard to believe they have the same parents.

Dogs are the same way. Far from being cut from the same furry cloth, every dog has a unique personality and temperament. The same types of discipline that work wonders with one dog may have no effect on another. It's not uncommon for people to diligently try to teach their dogs what they need to know, only to give up because they're convinced the dogs are incorrigible.

"I have seen owners tolerating terrible situations," says Ian Dunbar, Ph.D., a certified applied animal behaviorist in Berkeley, California. "They'll say things like, 'Well, he's just tricky with bones' or 'He doesn't really like kids.'"

It's fine to make allowances for dogs' individual differences and learning styles, but some types of misbehavior, such as aggression, are too serious to ignore—or handle on your own. "If you can't get the dog to stop what he's doing, it's time to call a behaviorist or find a proper trainer," says Dr. Dunbar. Some behavior problems will never get better without some help from a professional. In fact, they're almost certain to get worse, he adds.

Consider a technique called the alpha roll. People were often advised to reprimand their dogs by rolling them over onto their backs and forcing them to stay that way. It's a physically uncomfortable position. It's emotionally uncomfortable, as well, because it forces dogs into a submissive posture.

Choke collars are another way of meting out punishment. They're designed to pull tight when people pull on the leash. They put pressure on dogs' necks and immediately let them know when they're doing something wrong. There's nothing wrong with choke collars when they're properly used, and many trainers still recommend them. All too often, however, people were told to pull the collars very tight—tight enough to reduce or cut off the flow of air—whenever their dogs barked, jumped on people, tugged on the leash, or did anything else that "deserved" a swift correction.

Most experts today have a very dim view of these old-style training methods—not just because they were harsh but also because the theories that gave rise to them were largely wrong. It's true, for example, that dogs look up to their leaders; and those leaders, in traditional packs, could be tough disciplinarians. But alpha dogs weren't merely tough guys, says Dr. Dunbar. "Top-ranking dogs will often give gifts or share with lower-ranking dogs," he explains. "They most often rule by mental control, not physical aggression."

More important, experts came to realize what should have been obvious all along: Dogs are intelligent, sensitive animals who don't deserve physical punishment. In fact, they respond a lot better to praise and kindness.

Teaching dogs is easy because their natural inclination is to please. They just need to know what we want—and what we don't.

Gentle Discipline

Anyone who spends time around dogs knows how eager they are to please. They love food and adore going for walks, but what they crave most is the love and approval of their owners. Once they understand what people want, they'll do their best to deliver, says Dr. Hetts. Whether you're teaching basic obedience or correcting mistakes, you'll get the best results when you help your dog understand exactly what you want from her. Punishing bad behavior simply isn't necessary.

Teach what's good. Even though dogs have lived with humans for thousands of years, they have urges and agendas that are very different from ours. Their natural impulse is to do what they think is right, and they figure that everyone has the same idea as they do about what is "right." Once they understand that people expect something different, they're more than happy to oblige.

Suppose, for example, you're teaching your dog to walk on a leash. Rather than yanking the leash when she does the dog thing and goes the wrong way, help her understand that she's supposed to be following you. "Every 20 yards, stand still and ask your dog to sit," says Dr. Dunbar. "Don't move until she sits. Then say 'Good girl!' and perhaps give her a treat. Eventually, you will find that your dog sits whenever you stop walking because she understands that you're in control when she's on the leash."

Ignore what's bad. Dogs aren't angels. They're always doing things that they shouldn't, either because they don't know any better or because the temptation is too great to resist. Either way, punishment isn't necessary. In fact, you don't have to pay any attention to the misbehavior. What you should do is immediately encourage your dog to do something that's right.

Suppose your dog likes to jump on people when they walk in the door. Rather than yanking back on her collar every time she does it, plan ahead. Before opening the door, tell her to sit. Wait a few seconds to make sure she stays, then give her a lot of praise and something to eat. Dogs aren't foolish. They'll quickly learn that certain types of behavior—in this case, sitting when people come to the door—get your approval, and they'll want to keep doing them.

Teach with friendship. "Let go of the notion that you have to totally dominate your dog," Dr. Dunbar says. Unless you're planning to show your dog or enter her in competitions, there's no reason to demand clocklike precision or total obedience. Dogs respond very well to kindness and patience as well as to fun, he says. As long as you're consistent in the things you ask them to do—never letting them on the couch, for example, as opposed to forbidding it sometimes, but not always—they'll try their best to do them. The rest of the time, you can pretty much relax.

FAST FIX Every dog has certain objects, treats, or even words that she loves better than anything else. Most dogs are passionate about food, of course. Some dogs love tennis balls. Others love rawhides or

It's never easy for dogs to concentrate when they're outside. Food is an excellent way to get their attention. This Samoyed has learned to focus on his owner because she gives him treats when he does what she asks.

chasing sticks or having their ears stroked. Make a list of all the things your dog truly loves. Then, when you want to teach her something new or reward her for doing a great job, bring out one of her favorite rewards, says Dr. Dunbar. The good thing about making a list of 10 or 20 items is that you'll be able to rotate through the list so that every reward, rather than being used all the time, becomes something rare and special—and worth working for.

You can even use the *idea* of rewards to help dogs behave better. Every dog has a favorite word, like "ball" or "cookie." When you want them to stop doing something, say their favorite words. They'll rivet their attention on you, knowing they're about to get something good. And that's when you give the reward.

Dogs learn very quickly when they anticipate getting something good. For many dogs, that's food. For this collie mix, it's a game of ball.

Love and Protection

Beagles were bred to hunt small game, but they're better known for their pleasant personalities and rather intense loyalties. Even among beagles, however, Jack was a standout. A 6-year-old beagle in South Bend, Indiana, Jack took it upon himself to be the guide, protector, and even the eyes of his less fortunate companion.

Jane Amos, a trainer and groomer as well as Jack's owner, is extremely knowledgeable about dogs. But even she was surprised when Jack took a personal interest in assisting Tina, a diminutive and elderly miniature poodle who had lost her sight because of a detached retina.

"I didn't train him to do it, but one day, I began noticing that he was taking care of Tina," Amos says. "Jack would periodically look around the house for Tina to check on her and make sure she was doing okay. He even developed a method of nudging her and guiding her so that she would walk around obstacles and avoid bumping into things."

Beagles are small dogs who don't weigh much more than a small sack of kibble, but what they lack in size they make up for in spunk. Jack didn't hesitate to protect Tina from other, bigger dogs in the neighborhood. During walks, in fact, he would quickly change position to put himself between Tina and other dogs they happened to meet, and he'd stay there until the coast was clear, Amos says.

Tina eventually passed away, but during her last years, Jack never quit looking out for her. He didn't need any encouragement at all. Tina was always grateful for the help—and that was the only reward Jack wanted.

STRANGE behavior

Name SHELBY

Breed AUSTRALIAN SHEPHERD

Age 4

The Behavior

Morning comes early in Shelby's home. At least, it does for Shelby. About 10 minutes before the first alarm clock buzzes—and a full hour before the last wake-up call—Shelby starts working her way through the house. She's awake, and she wants everyone else to be awake, too. Her technique isn't subtle. She jumps up, puts her front feet on the beds, and barks. And licks. And nudges. If none of these does the trick, a cold nose usually does. No one in the house is an early riser, so Shelby's attentions aren't appreciated at all. Especially because they spent a lot of money for a dog door so she could let herself out. She never uses it in the morning because she doesn't have to go out. She just wants everyone up. And she's creative in making sure they get up.

The Solution

Dogs have internal alarm clocks that are every bit as precise as the clocks that people use. Shelby's clock, unfortunately, is set unusually early, and for good reason: She was bred to work and herd—and herding dogs don't lie around until noon.

"Aussies are very intelligent and work-oriented," says Kathleen Murnan, D.V.M., a veterinarian in Bedford, Texas. "They can learn to do just about anything, but sometimes if you don't give them a job, they'll make one up for themselves."

Shelby knows that people need to get up and get going in the morning, and she just wants to pitch in and help. Somehow, she got the idea that her job was to be a four-legged alarm clock, and she's not about to lie down on the job.

In a way, Shelby's people are lucky, says Dr. Murnan. Her internal clock is set close to the time of the first alarm; it could have been much earlier. Either way, Shelby isn't going to sleep any later. The only solution will be to convince her that she has done her job—before she actually wakes everyone up.

"The first person up can keep Shelby with him by giving her a bone, a toy to play with, or even having her sit in the bathroom while he grabs a shower," says Dr. Murnan. "When it's time for the next member of the family to get up, then the early riser can release Shelby and let her do her thing."

17

PART TWO

THE CIVIL DOG

In choosing to cast their lots with humans, dogs were rewarded with comfortable homes, great food, and the kind of pampering their wild ancestors couldn't have dreamed of. The trade-off is that we expect them to live by our rules—rules that are confusing and, well, completely undoglike. They'll never learn not to bolt their food or to abstain from sniffing strangers, but they can learn to be a little graceful in their human homes.

CHAPTER FOUR

SETTING RULES

When dogs do the wrong thing, it's often because they're not sure what the right thing is. People easily adjust to changing situations, but dogs don't. Consistent rules give them the chance to shine.

In 1998, syndicated newspaper columnist William Thomas wrote a piece about dog rules. With tongue firmly in cheek, he looked at how our efforts to set rules for our dogs often end up backfiring. The core of his column went something like this.

• The dog is not allowed in the house.

• Okay, the dog is allowed in the house, but only in certain rooms.

• The dog is allowed in all rooms, but has to stay off the furniture.

• All right, the dog can get on the old furniture only.

• Fine, the dog is allowed on all the furniture, but isn't allowed to sleep in the bed.

• Okay, the dog is allowed in bed, but only by invitation.

• The dog can sleep on the bed whenever he wants, but not under the covers.

• The dog can sleep under the covers by invitation only.

• The dog can sleep under the covers every night.

• Humans must ask permission to sleep under the covers with the dog.

Thanks to the speed of the Internet, various versions of Thomas's column flew around the world, appearing on dozens of Web sites and getting e-mailed to countless dog owners.

"It really hit a nerve," says Thomas, who writes from his home in Port Colborne, Ontario, Canada. "It rings so true in most people's experience."

Thomas's inspiration for the column came from his own dog, Jake, who was the first puppy he'd had since he was a kid. Having been a cat owner in the years between, Thomas learned anew how setting rules requires patience, dedication, and, above all, tenacity.

Any dog with an ounce of common sense will gravitate to a comfortable place. This fox terrier was allowed on the furniture once. Now she thinks she owns it.

"At every juncture, if you're not careful, you surrender—and pretty soon he's driving the car," says Thomas.

Why Rules?

While it's amusing to ponder how our dogs tend to train us instead of the other way around, the reality is a little more serious. "How many dogs are a pain in the neck most of the time when they could be great friends almost all of the time?" says Jeff Nichol, D.V.M., a veterinarian at the Adobe Animal Medical Center in Albuquerque, New Mexico.

People value freedom in their lives, and they assume that freedom is good for their dogs, as well. But dogs don't do well with too much freedom. In fact, they crave discipline, says Joanne Howl, D.V.M., a veterinarian in West River, Maryland.

"It is vital to their basic nature as pack animals that they have rules," she explains.

When you set rules and enforce them, you're establishing a very important role for yourself—that of the leader. If you don't set rules, your dog will feel that she has no other choice but to move into the leadership void and start setting the rules herself. That's about the time when everyone stops getting along.

People tend to view their dogs as being equal members of the family. Dogs, on the other hand, never see people (or other dogs) as equals. There are always differences in the pack hierarchy. This means that if you're not at the top of

Labradors like to chew sticks, and this Lab mix is no exception. His owners encourage it, so he knows it's okay. Clear expectations make dogs happy—almost as happy as sticks do.

the family pack, your dog will see you as being below her—and her behavior will reflect this.

On the other hand, when you set rules and are firm about enforcing them, your dog's behavior will reflect this, too. "Dogs are not only comfortable with being subservient to the leader, that's a fundamental part of their nature," says Dr. Nichol.

The Canine Commandments

So what rules are important? One thing to remember is that what may be an important rule for one dog isn't necessarily important for another. And the same is true of owners. One person may not give a hoot when her dog

This Border collie pup is learning that she has to work before she can play. She'll happily sit—as long as she gets to run afterward.

climbs on the furniture; for someone else, this may be a major infraction.

Still, there are a few rules that every dog should be expected to follow. You can think of these as Canine Commandments. Other rules, which will vary among dogs and owners, are more along the lines of local ordinances.

Thou shalt come when called. It's not that big a deal if your dog doesn't roll over when you tell her to, but "come" is one command that should get an immediate, no-questions-asked response. Dogs who are running toward traffic—

or, more often, toward unsuspecting people—can get in a lot of trouble. "You have an obligation to be able to keep your dog under control," says Dr. Nichol.

Thou shalt honor thy grandmother. Experts in animal behavior often refer to a rule called Granny's rule. Also known as no free lunches, Granny's rule basically means that for every good thing you do for your dog, she has to do something to earn it. "This is a guiding principle of dog training," says Mark Plonsky, Ph.D., professor of psychology at the University of Wisconsin at Stevens Point and a canine behavioral consultant.

Granny's rule is critical because it establishes you as the person your dog needs to listen to. Dogs respond to Granny's rule because it also operates very strongly among dogs, where all good things came from the leader. What works among dogs also works when people enter the equation. When you give your dog her food, for example, she should always be required to sit and wait quietly until you let her know it's okay to eat. When you're getting ready to play catch or take her for a walk, have her perform a small trick or respond to a certain command.

Thou shalt not growl at thy leader. Sometimes it's hard to keep from laughing when dogs grumble at people who walk too close to their food bowls, or growl when people try to pry shoes from their mouths. But this type of behavior isn't cute, because it invariably leads to problems. A dog would never growl at her pack leader, Dr. Howl explains. Dogs only growl at people when they're challenging their leadership. "A leader needs to stand tall," she says. "If the leader is upset, a properly trained dog will

This shiba inu is acknowledging her owner's leadership by rolling over and showing her belly in a gesture of respectful submission.

drop lower to the ground. If a leader is really upset, a dog will roll over and show her belly."

One way to establish your role as the leader is to literally be the top dog—with the emphasis on top. Hold yourself high when you approach your dog, says Dr. Howl. When you're playing, make sure your dog is physically lower than you are. Dogs automatically respect size, and they'll pick up on the fact that your imposing stature is that of a leader.

Thou shalt follow the leader. How many times have you opened the door only to get shoved aside as your dog barrels out? And how many people try in vain to wedge their legs in front of their eager dogs when visitors come to the door? Dogs who rush past people are showing serious disrespect, says Dr. Howl. Once again, the reason for this can be traced to their days in packs. The leader was the one who left the den first; other, lower-ranking dogs followed.

What kept the peace in packs will also keep the peace in human families, explains Dr. Howl. Your job is to lead the way. Your dog's job is to follow close behind.

Enforcing the Rules

Dog are a lot like children in some ways. They test you. They push the boundaries of the rules you set, especially in the first 2 years of life. People need to see this time as their dogs' adolescence—and adolescents always need firm and consistent rules to follow.

Before setting rules, however, you have to decide which ones are actually important enough to enforce. There's not much point in laying down edicts if you're not prepared to back them up. In fact, rules that don't get enforced send a powerful message that it's okay for dogs to ignore more important rules.

Families aren't run like military units, of course. The idea isn't for people to be sergeants and dogs to be the raw recruits. But you do want to be consistent. Rather than setting dozens of rules that may be time-consuming and difficult

BREED SPECIFIC

All dogs need rules, but some breeds need them more than others. Border collies and Australian shepherds (left) have been bred to interact closely with the people in their lives. As a result, they're constantly asking for direction and feedback. More than most breeds, they need their owners to clearly communicate what is expected. When they don't get clear directions, they may feel as though they're failing.

23

to enforce, you may decide you only need two or three. The number isn't important; enforcing them consistently is.

Write them down. People make up rules all the time—and change them just as often. That's fine when you're dealing with other adults, but it's confusing as heck for dogs. Make a list of the rules you want your dog to know, Dr. Nichol recommends. So you don't forget—and to remind other people in the family—post the list somewhere obvious, like on the refrigerator door. "You need to be clear about what your dog is expected to do, especially if there is more than one person in the family," says Dr. Nichol.

Bring others to the bowl. It's common for dogs to listen to one person in the family and ignore everyone else. One solution is to have other people in the family feed your dog while the "top dog" stands by, suggests Dr. Plonsky. And before she gets the food, have her sit quietly or obey a command or two. When she gets the idea that all the people in the family have the power to control her food supply, she'll understand that all people need to be listened to.

PUPPY DOG TALES

The Dog Who Beat the Machines

Peaches, a nearly all-white beagle, earned her living by smelling wood-destroying termites. Her reputation as a bug-busting miracle spread, resulting in a challenge: She would be pitted against human pest inspectors as well as high-tech detection devices.

The contest was to be held at a building in State College, Pennsylvania, that had known termite activity, says Robert Snetsinger, Ph.D., professor emeritus of entomology at Pennsylvania State University in University Park. "We went to the Park Forest Village Community Church, which was a beautiful, older wooden building, and I checked it out carefully. I knew where we'd had recent swarms and where the termites were living."

While a dog's nose can't be patented as a new invention, it is a miracle device that boggles the modern mind. A beagle's nose has over 30 times as much skin devoted to scenting as does a human's. The olfactory bulb, the smell-center in the brain, is four times bigger than a person's.

"Peaches and I had been working together for about 2 years when I got a letter inviting us to the contest," says Mike Del Gaudio, former owner of a pest-control business in Scranton, Pennsylvania. "I knew she was good, but getting asked to prove it in front of all my peers was pretty scary."

He needn't have worried. At the command "termites," Peaches started to quiver. Her head cocked and her brown eyes glowed. As the machines slowly and mechanically combed the building, Peaches just kept finding bugs. "We hit on a couple of areas that were thought to be termite-free," Mike says. "Well, they weren't bug-free. When they opened the area to visual inspection later, there were nice infestations of destructive carpenter ants."

Peaches quickly found all the termites that the judges knew were there, plus an additional 12 sites that no one had known about. In short, she blew the doors off her competition.

Mike basked in the accolades for a few minutes, then slipped away to celebrate privately. "I took her to lunch, and she scarfed down three chili dogs," he says.

Dogs need to understand that all the people in the family are higher in status than they are, including the children.

Provide a place for time-outs. You can't be around your dog all the time. For puppies especially, time spent alone is often time spent acquiring bad habits. People are often reluctant to teach their dogs to stay in crates, but it's probably the best way to minimize problems while also making dogs feel safe and secure. "It's like a wolf's den," says Dr. Plonsky. "This is the den that your dog's wild ancestors would dig to take a nap. It's not a prison, but a very comfortable place to be."

FAST FIX People tend to underestimate how much exercise dogs really need. Whether you have a slothful Great Dane or a Border collie dynamo, regular exercise is the only way to help her burn off energy. Dogs who don't exercise enough tend to get restless and bored. Dogs who are bored tend to get stubborn and distracted.

Dogs need at least 20 minutes of exercise twice a day. Some breeds, like terriers and herding dogs, may need as much as a few hours. People who have been dealing with behavior problems are often amazed at how much their dogs improve once they get their paws moving. Walking around the park or chasing balls gives dogs the mental stimulation and social interaction they crave. Exercise also tires them out, and tired dogs are the best-behaved dogs.

Kelpies are working dogs who need tremendous amounts of exercise to feel—and act—good.

25

CHAPTER FIVE

CONSISTENCY COUNTS

Dogs want to please the people in their lives, but they get confused when something that's allowed one day gets them into trouble the next. Giving clear and consistent messages is the best way to help them understand what they're supposed to do.

We appreciate consistency in our lives. We demand it in our peanut butter. We treasure it when our paychecks arrive on time. And we like the fact that the supermarket always has what we're looking for when we stop by after work.

The consistency that we value for ourselves, however, doesn't always carry over to our dogs. "We complain about our dogs begging at the table, but then we turn around and slip them some food when we're in a generous mood," says Amy Marder, V.M.D., clinical assistant professor at Tufts University School of Veterinary Medicine in North Grafton, Massachusetts, and vice president of behavioral medicine and companion-animal services at the American Society for the Prevention of Cruelty to Animals in New York City. Or we encourage them to jump up and greet us when we're wearing old clothes, but then flip out when they do the same thing when we're wearing new suits.

Meanwhile, our dogs' feelings about all of these mixed messages can be summed up in one word: "Huh?"

A World That Makes Sense

Dogs are very smart animals who can understand and anticipate a lot of the things that we do. But unless you keep to a regular schedule and respond consistently to certain types of

A dog who scores at the supper table once is going to keep coming back for more.

behavior, you're asking them to learn things that their brains aren't built to deal with—mainly, the idea of appropriateness. Dogs can't understand that an action that's acceptable at one time isn't at another. They don't factor in things like your mood, your clothes, or the fact that Aunt Ruth has a morbid fear of dogs.

"We try to make dogs think like people, and it just doesn't work," says Norma C. Guy, D.V.M., a veterinary behaviorist with the Atlantic Veterinary College in Charlottetown, Prince Edward Island, Canada. People spend many years learning the nuances of appropriate behavior. Dogs don't and can't. Without clear and consistent guidelines, they have a hard time figuring out what they're supposed to do. This can lead to a huge amount of confusion, and the more confused dogs get, the harder it is for them to behave in ways we appreciate. This in turn makes them anxious, says Dr. Guy. Dogs crave predictability, and when things aren't predictable, they get tense and unhappy.

"It can be next to impossible to stop bad behavior if you're not being consistent," adds Joanne Howl, D.V.M., a veterinarian in West River, Maryland. It doesn't matter whether you're trying to stop your dog from begging at the table or encouraging him to be more sedate around visitors. Giving clear and consistent messages will help him learn more quickly and remember what he learned.

Get everyone with the program. If you live alone with your dog, it's pretty easy to be consistent. It's not so easy when there are other people in the family, each of whom may be giving a different message. "Dogs know how to manipulate the person who is most easily ma-

The same body clocks that tell dogs when their owners are coming home also make them sticklers for punctuality and routine.

nipulated," says Dr. Howl. No matter how strict you are about not feeding your dog from the table, for example, he's going to keep mooching if someone else is slipping him strips of bacon.

The easiest way to prevent mixed messages is to get everyone together and come up with a list of things that everyone agrees with, like certain types of behavior that will always be discouraged, says Karen L. Overall, V.M.D., Ph.D., a certified animal behaviorist and director of the behavior clinic at the University of Pennsylvania School of Veterinary Medicine in Philadelphia.

Live day to day. Dogs learn best when the same things happen at the same times every day, says Dr. Guy. Whereas people view weeks, months, and years as significant milestones, for dogs, these long periods of time mean squat. They simply don't have long memories. On the other hand, their internal clocks are exceptionally accurate. That's why your dog goes to the door minutes before you come home from work. He knows that you'll be walking in soon because his inner alarm clock tells him so.

"A daily routine really helps relieve anxiety," says Dr. Guy. She recommends feeding dogs at the same time every day, going for walks at the same time, and setting up consistent training times. Dogs feel more confident when things are on schedule, and happy dogs are much less likely to do things that people don't like, such as chewing apart the couch cushions.

No means no. No one enjoys being the disciplinarian. When you're tired at the end of the day, it's not a lot of fun to struggle with an obstinate dog. This is why it's easy to let things slide. You may have told your dog a dozen times to get off the couch, but he keeps creeping up, and finally you give up.

Bad choice, says Dr. Overall. This type of inconsistency teaches dogs that it's okay to ignore commands. Like boorish suitors, they get the idea that when you say "no,"

they just have to try a little harder to get what they want.

Commands such as "no," "sit," and "get off the couch" shouldn't be negotiating points, says Dr. Overall. You have to be unfailingly consistent in enforcing them. "If you do this one simple thing, you won't have to be a disciplinarian all the time," she says. Your dog will understand what you want, and he'll accept your rules. And he'll be happier because there's less confusion in his life.

FAST FIX We spend so much time with our dogs that we often assume we're all speaking the same language. Research has shown, in fact, that 24 percent of owners believe that their dogs understand everything they say. But a lot of the time, dogs don't understand. Dogs are capable of learning dozens of words, but they have a hard time distinguishing words that are similar but not identical to the words that they do know. That's why a dog may respond beautifully to a word such as "come," but will look totally confused when he hears variations such as "c'mere" and "come on, boy."

"When you do that, your dog has to relearn the phrase," says Dr. Howl. That's why veterinarians recommend that you use exactly the same words all the time. When your dog doesn't have to guess what you're saying, he will be much more likely to respond quickly and with pleasure, she says.

BREED SPECIFIC

Every dog benefits from having a lot of consistency in his life, but large breeds with the most exuberance, like Labrador retrievers (right), absolutely require it in order to control their friendly, but sometimes over-the-top, energy.

STRANGE behavior

Name STORMY

Breed LABRADOR RETRIEVER

Age 2

The Behavior

Stormy doesn't drink his water, he plays with it. Every time his owners fill his bowl, Stormy takes a few sips, then puts his front feet in the dish and begins splashing water all over the place, making one heck of a mess. His owners are facing a frustrating dilemma. They're sick and tired of cleaning up the spills after Stormy's perpetual water baths, but they don't want him to go thirsty because there isn't any water left in the bowl.

So far, they've decided to keep the bowl full, or at least try to, but the kitchen floor is starting to get waterlogged. They've tried using a weighted dish that's harder to tip over, but Stormy manages to spill all the water anyway.

The Solution

"This dog wants to swim," says Judith Halliburton, a trainer and behaviorist in Albuquerque, New Mexico, and author of *Raising Rover*. "He's a Labrador and it's in his blood, just like fetching. Labs have been bred for hundreds of years to work in the water, and they naturally enjoy it."

Even Labradors can learn to be a little neater, she adds—but the only way this is going to happen is if Stormy satisfies his water jones somewhere else. If they have a good-sized backyard, Stormy's owners could buy a small kiddie pool. "Stick it in the yard, fill it half-full, and let him have at it," Halliburton says. "Even in cooler weather, he may decide to go for a dip; and in warm weather, he'll probably live in it."

A more convenient solution would be for Stormy's owners to drop by a pet supply store and buy an elevated food-and-water stand. Usually made from stainless steel or plastic, this type of stand raises the bowls off the floor to about mouth level. Although they're mainly used to make eating easier for dogs with joint problems, raising the water 1 to 2 feet off the ground will ensure that Stormy doesn't stand in it.

"Lastly, when he's had his drink and starts messing around, take the bowl away," Halliburton says. "When he's calm and behaving again, put it back. He'll soon get the idea that the water in his dish is just a beverage, not a plaything."

CHAPTER SIX

REWARD THE GOOD

Dogs thrive on positive feedback. Rewarding them for doing the right thing works better than correcting them for causing trouble. Dogs are happiest and most confident when they get lots of praise—and know that they've earned it.

Ralph Waldo Emerson said, "The only reward of virtue is virtue." One thing is certain: He was not talking about dogs.

People who expect their dogs to naturally gravitate towards virtuous behavior, wearing nothing but a smile, are in for some disappointment. "It's not that dogs are selfish or inherently bad. It's just that they perceive things differently than we do," says Joanne Howl, D.V.M., a veterinarian in West River, Maryland. Dogs essentially see the world in one of three ways. Things are either good, bad, or indifferent, and these perceptions govern everything that they do.

- Things that are good are those that bear rewards, such as food, affection, and fun. Dogs naturally gravitate back to these things.

- Bad things are those that have unpleasant consequences, like a bitter taste or a porcupine quill in the nose. Dogs learn to avoid these things.
- Things that dogs are indifferent to, well, they just don't register on the radar, and dogs don't waste any brain space thinking about them.

For a long time, trainers and behaviorists believed that the best way to teach dogs good manners was to manipulate their instinct to avoid the bad. Dogs who ignored commands, rooted through the trash can, or otherwise got out of line were scolded or given a quick swat, says Norma C. Guy, D.V.M., a veterinary behaviorist with the Atlantic Veterinary College in Charlottetown, Prince Edward Island, Canada. The idea was that they'd associate the bad experience with the bad behavior, and this would put them on the path to righteousness.

There's certainly some truth to this. Imagine that you're a dog and you've just come across a skunk. Blam, you get a shot of staggering stink right in your snout. The next time you see a skunk, you'll be afraid that it will happen again, and you'll wisely take a detour because you now associate skunks with pain and misery.

But suppose you're lying quietly at home, happily munching on this great-tasting leather thing. You don't know that it cost $300 and came from Italy. All you know is that all of a sudden you got a tremendous wallop from your human. Sure, you now associate leather shoes with pain, but you also see your owner in a new, and not altogether pleasant, light.

"It's completely inappropriate to train an unwanted behavior out of a dog with punishment," says Dr. Guy. Dogs who are often punished may become anxious and fearful, and this causes them to act in anxious and fearful ways—which generates even more discipline. "It becomes a vicious cycle," she says.

I Like It When You Praise Me

Behaviorists have discovered that dogs learn better and faster when they're rewarded for good behavior rather than punished for bad. The good feelings that come from rewards last a long time, and the desire to repeat those feelings encourages dogs to keep doing well, says Dr. Howl. At the same time, dogs who are rewarded for doing good things feel closer to their owners and are less afraid than those who are always getting punished.

Rewarding good behavior doesn't mean pampering dogs or giving them crunchy biscuits just because they look cute when they're sleeping in the sun. It does mean giving them positive feedback when they do something that you want them to do. Suppose your dog is barking and you tell him to stop. He stops, and you give him a reward. It won't take him long to figure out that being quiet and listening to commands gets him a treat, while barking doesn't get him much of anything at all.

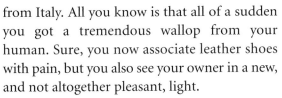

Dogs learn by associating actions with results. An action that brings pleasant results—such as a pat and some praise in return for not nosing visitors—is one that they will be eager to repeat.

Timing is everything. Dogs are natural Zen Buddhists in the sense that they live mainly in the moment. Their memories simply aren't very good. That's why it's no use giving them rewards for something they did in the past—and for dogs, the present becomes the past after a few seconds. They'll gladly gobble up the treat, but they won't have a clue what it's for, says Liz Palika, a trainer in Oceanside, California, and author of *All Dogs Need Some Training*. "If you even wait 10 seconds to reward them for doing something good, it's too late," she says.

Of course, dogs who are in the process of learning proper behavior don't have a lot of successes at first. You'll probably need to follow them around just to catch them doing something right. Maybe your dog sniffs your slippers and walks on without touching them. Immediately praise him to high heaven and slip him a treat, says Palika. Does he look at the garbage can and decline to dig through it, or curl up on the carpet instead of on the couch? Let your voice be heard and the biscuit box be emptied.

Customize the rewards. Even though most dogs believe that food is the best reward they'll ever get, it's not the only reward or even the best one. For one thing, dogs tend to put on weight, and you don't want to beef them up, no matter how good they are. And some dogs are equally motivated by praise, toys, or other kinds of rewards. "You really need to take the personality and breed of the dog into consideration," says Palika.

Sight hounds such as Afghans and greyhounds were bred for hunting and chasing small animals, and they usually appreciate squeaky

Some dogs aren't motivated much by food. The promise of a game has this kelpie's attention and may be the most effective inducement to good behavior.

toys they can chew on. "Terriers go bonkers over fuzzy mouse toys," says Palika. Bred for hunting rodents, they like the feeling of furlike material in their mouths, she explains. Herding dogs such as Australian shepherds and Border collies won't say no to food, but a quick tear around the backyard, with you running behind and shouting praises, will have even more impact.

"If you're having trouble finding something, take your dog to the pet supply store and walk him up and down the aisles a few times," suggests Palika. Make the circuit through the cat section, too, since many dogs—especially digging dogs such as dachshunds—love toys that are shaped like rodents. Let your dog sniff the offerings. Hold toys in front of him and see what he likes. When he shows a lot of interest, you'll know you've found a special toy.

Reward little and well. Just as children who grow up having ice cream for supper may start feeling entitled to it, dogs lose the meaning behind treats when they get them too often, says Amy Marder, V.M.D., clinical assistant professor at Tufts University School of Veterinary Medicine in North Grafton, Massachusetts, and vice president of behavioral medicine and companion-animal services at the American Society for the Prevention of Cruelty to Animals in New York City. Overindulgence is fine at first, Dr. Marder adds. You want to reward your dog a lot when he's learning new things. After a few weeks, it's time to taper off. Rather than giving a reward every time he does something right, give it every second or third time, she suggests. Within a few months, the good behavior will become habitual. At that point, only hand over rewards occasionally.

You can tell if you're rewarding your dog too often by watching his reactions. The sight or smell of a treat should generate a lot of enthusiasm. If he gives you a ho-hum kind of look, you'll know you're being too generous. Or maybe it's time to switch to a reward that *does* get him excited.

Help him succeed. Some dogs just can't seem to get it right. Maybe you say "sit", and your dog gives the blankest look you've ever seen. You tell him to get off the couch, and he merely stretches and sighs. You wait eagerly, treat in hand, for him to do something—anything—right so that you can reward him. Meanwhile, he happily chews your shoes or lifts his leg on your rubber boots.

You can't wait forever, says Dr. Guy. Sometimes, it's better to be a role model and walk your dog through the proper behavior. "If you catch him in midstream, pick him up and take him outside and let him finish," she says. "Then reward him there." Try this technique anytime you find your dog doing something that he shouldn't.

Suppose you find him with his head buried in the trash. Take him by the collar and gently walk him past the trash a couple of times without letting him stop or sniff. Lead him to

PUPPY DOG TALES

On the Money

David Baca of Embudo, New Mexico, doesn't worry about rewarding his dog, Oliver. That's because Oliver, a Pekingese–pug mix, takes care of that all on his own. And if he's feeling particularly generous, he may reward his owner as well.

Oliver has a gift for ferreting out money. While other dogs dream of filet mignon or chasing rabbits, Oliver is most likely dreaming up his next big score. Baca discovered Oliver's affinity for greenbacks when a girlfriend began complaining that she was missing money. For three weeks, Baca kept getting blamed for her financial losses. But since he was broke at the time and was also short a few $5 bills himself, he couldn't figure out what was happening with the cash.

One day on a hunch, Baca set a $10 bill on the coffee table and stepped around a corner to watch. Sure enough, Oliver picked up the money. After following Oliver around for a while, Baca discovered an extra $45 stashed behind the refrigerator.

Oliver's heists made sense considering Baca's earlier days as a cattle rancher and his forays into town. When he and Oliver would walk past Zeller's General Store in town, he would occasionally slip Oliver some cash. Oliver would hold the bills in his mouth and walk into the store. Clerks in the store who knew Oliver would take the cash and give him a can of Vienna sausages, which he'd carry outside. Baca would open the can and give the frankfurters to Oliver—and that's a lesson no dog is going to forget.

another room, then reward and praise him there, says Dr. Guy. He'll begin to understand that certain types of behavior—walking past the trash, ignoring the shoes, staying off the couch—bring him the things he loves.

CHAPTER SEVEN

IGNORE THE BAD

Attention is a powerful reward. Dogs prefer positive, happy attention,
but they'll settle for the negative kind. That's why ignoring bad
behavior is often more effective than punishing it.

Every elementary school classroom has a kid who jumps up in the middle of a lesson and does an impromptu dance. Who makes grotesque faces. Who is always practicing armpit noises. "Ignore him," teachers say. "He's just looking for attention."

Animal behaviorists can relate to this. Some dogs are the canine equivalents of classroom cutups. And the solution is often the same, says Mary Lee Nitschke, Ph.D., an animal behavior therapist in Portland, Oregon. By ignoring some of your dog's less pleasing manners, you're taking away that which she holds most dear: your attention. "This is probably the most powerful tool people have in their training repertoires," says Dr. Nitschke.

Imagine dogs in the wild. In each pack, there's an alpha dog who is the leader. When a lower-ranking dog does something annoying or troublesome, the regal alpha dog doesn't even bother to look her way. It's only when a dog does something the alpha dog likes that she gets rewarded with his attention, says Karen L. Overall, V.M.D., Ph.D.,

a certified animal behaviorist and director of the behavior clinic at the University of Pennsylvania School of Veterinary Medicine in Philadelphia.

In human families, the alpha dog is you. And you can use your status as leader to help your dog behave better. "The way to correct a dog for poor behavior is not to punish her," Dr. Overall says. "You withdraw your attention."

When to Ignore

Ignoring bad behavior isn't a panacea, of course. It doesn't work at all when dogs are doing something aggressive or highly physical, if only because they're probably not paying attention to

BREED SPECIFIC

Ignoring bad behavior works best with dogs who have been bred to form very deep bonds with their owners, such as Siberian huskies and Alaskan malamutes (left). On the other hand, dogs who bond with everyone, like Labrador retrievers, are less likely to respond to this technique.

you when they're that worked up, says Bob Gutierrez, animal-behavior coordinator at the San Francisco Society for the Prevention of Cruelty to Animals.

It also doesn't work when dogs are doing something they enjoy quite a bit, such as barking at butterflies or chasing cats across the yard. Your approval won't add one whit to their pleasure because the activity itself is so much fun. "They're enjoying themselves and having a great time, and that's their reward," Gutierrez says.

The cold shoulder works best as a teaching tool when dogs are misbehaving in ways that demand your attention, such as jumping up, begging, barking, or hand-nudging. This technique doesn't work immediately, Dr. Nitschke adds. When you do it consistently, however, it will teach a lesson that dogs can remember.

How to Ignore

It's easy enough to turn your back on your dog when she's misbehaving. But there's a fine line between teaching and punishing. Ignoring dogs for too long or doing it too often won't make them better behaved. It will make them anxious. The idea is to withdraw your attention only until they have stopped doing whatever it is that you want them to stop. Then you can turn on the charm again.

But don't actually praise them at that point, Dr. Nitschke says. That would be telling them that their hijinks will get your attention—if they wait long enough.

Look away. Dogs are intensely aware of eye contact. In their natural world, a direct look can be either an invitation or a threat. Either way, it conveys strong emotional messages. Dogs who are being pushy or pestering you for attention will always be checking your eyes to gauge your reaction. You can send a message back by pointedly not looking at them, which tells them you don't approve, says Dr. Nitschke.

Ignore them immediately. Dogs don't need a lot of encouragement to continue doing things. Hesitating for a moment when they bark to get your attention or jump on you when you walk through the door gives them a window of interaction that they crave. And so they'll keep doing it.

"Immediately turn around, put your hands in your pockets, and stare at the ceiling," says Dr. Nitschke. Dogs can read body language, and they recognize the cold shoulder when they see it. It's an effective way to show your disapproval and take the fun out of whatever it is they're doing, she explains.

This whippet mix jumps up because she wants some face time with her owner. Turning away and ignoring the behavior takes away the one thing she wants most, forcing her to choose another type of greeting.

35

Be strong. Dogs are like children in that they're very persistent and quick to take advantage of moments of weakness. Ignoring them for 5 seconds—or even 5 minutes—sends a powerful signal, but that doesn't mean they'll quit pushing. In fact, they invariably whine louder or push with their noses a little more. Giving in at this point can set you back for weeks. "What you've done is reward the escalated response," says Dr. Nitschke. "You've just taught your dog to persist."

 **FAST FIX** A quick way to let dogs know that you don't approve of what they're doing is to leave them by themselves, says Dr. Overall. Suppose your dog walks into the kitchen while you're talking with a guest and plops a wet, dirty tennis ball on the clean linoleum—an invitation to play catch. The two of you should stop talking and leave the room. "Your dog will start thinking, 'Gee, I got a lot more interaction when I left the ball outside,'" says Dr. Overall.

Jealousy is clearly an issue for this Maltese, who will keep pestering his owner until he gets some attention. By refusing to acknowledge his entreaties, his owner is showing him that his techniques aren't working and he'll need to try something else.

Stay in the present. No one enjoys coming home after work and discovering that the contents of several garbage cans have been strewn all over the house. This is the type of situation when good intentions—"I will ignore bad behavior; I will not go crazy"—tend to break down. But ignoring the behavior is the only thing you can do. Yelling or punishing dogs for things that happened hours before doesn't work. Your dog simply won't understand what you're mad about. She'll just know you're mad—and she'll get anxious because she won't understand why.

POOCH PUZZLER

Why do small dogs take up so much room on the bed?

People who allow their dogs in the beds are often amazed by the amount of space they take up. Especially when it's 3:00 A.M. and they're freely lounging over a portion of the comforter that's well beyond what their body sizes seem to require. The people in the bed, of course, are invariably curled into compact little balls.

Small dogs do take up more room relative to their size, says Bob Gutierrez, animal-behavior coordinator at the San Francisco Society for the Prevention of Cruelty to Animals. Small dogs give birth to small litters of one or two pups, he explains. Big dogs, on the other hand, have litters of five or six pups. To make room in the den for all their siblings, big dogs learned to sleep tightly curled up. But small dogs get used to having the joint to themselves or sharing it with just one sibling. So they naturally sprawl out and take all the room that's available.

STRANGE
behavior

Name HOPIE

Breed MINIATURE DACHSHUND

Age 4

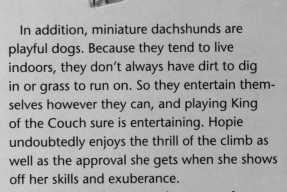

The Behavior Hopie is into height. The baby of the family, she pretty much has the run of the house. The floor doesn't interest her much—even though, as a dachshund, that's the area she's closest to. What she really likes is to get as high as she can, which usually means climbing on the furniture. She has gotten pretty good at it, and that's fine with her owners. But as soon as they turn their backs, she scampers even higher—onto the backs of sofas and armchairs, for example—and perches. When she's caught and confronted, she gets frightened and pees. No one really minds her escalating habit, but the upholstery is taking a beating from the moisture.

The Solution Quite a few dogs like perching in high spots. In the wild, dogs get up on rocks or banks so they can see what's going on around them and also to be safe from potential predators, says Betty Fisher, a trainer based in San Diego and co-author of *So Your Dog's Not Lassie*. "A lot of dogs, even much bigger ones, sit on the tops of furniture. It feels like a nice, safe place."

In addition, miniature dachshunds are playful dogs. Because they tend to live indoors, they don't always have dirt to dig in or grass to run on. So they entertain themselves however they can, and playing King of the Couch sure is entertaining. Hopie undoubtedly enjoys the thrill of the climb as well as the approval she gets when she shows off her skills and exuberance.

Hopie probably has another reason for getting up there, as well. Miniature dachshunds are quite small—you could tuck a few of them into a medium-size handbag. Getting on the top of the couch undoubtedly makes her feel taller and more confident. "I'd be willing to bet that Hopie is very sensitive and that she has accidents on the furniture only when she's getting yelled at and is afraid," says Fisher.

Since no one in the family seriously objects to Hopie's excursions, they should probably just relax and let her do it. Hopie doesn't shed a lot, and she's too small to cause much damage. Once she realizes that no one is going to yell at her, she'll quit watering the upholstery, Fisher says.

37

CHAPTER EIGHT

WHEN TO PRACTICE MANNERS

Education is a lifetime endeavor, which is why it has to be convenient
for people as well as dogs. Good timing is everything. Just try teaching
obedience after lunch—you'll both get failing grades.

There's one thing that explains the success of stock market moguls, stand-up comics, world-renowned watchmakers, and people who have the knack for boiling the perfect egg: They all have good timing.

Timing is equally important when you're teaching your dog to be a good citizen, says Quenten London, a training consultant with the National Institute of Dog Training in Los Angeles. In fact, knowing when to work with your dog is often as important as knowing what to work on. "You're the one who's right there when problems occur," London says.

On the Clock

From a human point of view, good timing is mainly about convenience. Promising yourself that you'll give your dog lessons every morning isn't very realistic if you have three children to get off to school and you can hardly get to work on time. It doesn't matter if your dog wakes up alert and ready to go unless you're alert and ready to go at the same time. That's why the best time to work with your dog ultimately depends on your schedule.

From a dog's point of view, good timing is simply predictable timing. Dogs love regular schedules, says Norma C. Guy, D.V.M., veterinary behaviorist at the Atlantic Veterinary College in Charlottetown, Prince Edward Island, Canada. Predictability makes their world more understandable and less stressful. And the more

This golden retriever knows to the minute when it's time for her regular walk, and has learned to lie down politely and wait for her owner's signal.

confident and relaxed they feel, the better they're going to learn, she explains.

Follow the clock. Even though dogs have a hazy concept of time, their body clocks are exceptionally accurate—which is why they can predict to the minute when you're getting ready to fill their food bowls. You can take advantage of their internal clocks—and their eagerness preceding regularly scheduled events—by practicing lessons at the same times every day, says Robert L. DeFranco, executive director of the Animal Behavior Center of New York, a nonprofit animal education and welfare organization in New York City. By the time you snap on their leashes and step outside, they'll be primed and ready to go, he explains.

Teach briefly and often. Dogs have very short attention spans, which is why long training sessions don't work, DeFranco says. They can stay alert and focused for about 20 minutes—and that's on a good day. Ten minutes is probably closer to the mark. Dogs can't learn a lot in 10 minutes, however, which is why most trainers recommend working with them two or three times a day, for 10 to 20 minutes each time.

When you miss a session, which happens all the time, don't bother making up for it by making the next session longer, DeFranco adds. Your dog will only lose interest—and, in most cases, so will you.

Teach first, feed later. Since food is such a powerful lure, the minutes before meals are

often the best times to give quick lessons, says Dr. Guy. For example, have your dog sit and lie down a few times before you put his bowl on the floor. Practice a few "stay" and "come" commands. These short lessons can be very efficient. "Most people just dump the food in the bowl and leave, which is unfortunate because mealtime is one of the best times for training," says Dr. Guy.

FAST FIX If school boards had a diabolical urge to reduce test scores by 10 points or so, all they'd have to do is give the exams after a heavy lunch. Dogs wouldn't do any better. A full dog is a lazy dog—one who would really like to stretch out for awhile. Listening to you won't be a high priority right

These dogs are learning that they can't start eating until their owner gives the command. The older dogs get full marks for trying, but the puppy in the foreground hasn't quite mastered the lesson.

after eating, says DeFranco. That's why you'll get the best results when you practice lessons before your dog has eaten.

Impromptu Teaching

Schedules are great when you're helping dogs learn the social fundamentals, but they're useless for dealing with breakdowns in behavior that are unanticipated or occur at random times. Suppose, for example, your dog has gotten into the habit of raiding the trash. Sure, you can scold him at 5:50 P.M. when you get home from work. He'll listen respectfully and maybe cock his head. The next day, he'll rummage through the trash again because he didn't have a clue what you were talking about.

Compared to people, dogs have very short attention spans. Punishing them hours after a particular misdeed has no effect because they can't possibly remember what they did. Your window of opportunity to instill good manners is only a few minutes long. "You have to modify the behavior as it's occurring," explains London.

The problem, of course, is that dogs are not stupid. Even though they probably don't plan their day's mischief ahead of time, they do recognize ripe opportunities when they see them. That's why they never tip over the trash can when you're standing in the kitchen with them, but they gleefully empty the contents and drag the can around the house when you're away at work. It's a Catch-22: Scolding them later doesn't work, and you're never around to catch them in the act.

There is a way around this: You have to lead them into temptation at a time when you're

Parks and outdoor areas are full of interesting distractions. This bull terrier mix needs to learn to ignore them and to focus on her owner instead.

going to be home and watching. Suppose your dog is an incorrigible trashmonger. On a day when you've thrown away some particularly redolent scraps, leave the lid off the can and leave the house—but don't go far. Walk around the block, water the flowers, and generally give your dog a little time to get ideas. Then quickly come back in. If you're lucky, you'll find him with his head neck-deep in the can. At that point, you can scold him and put him in a room by himself for a few minutes. He'll know exactly what he did and why you're angry, and that's a powerful combination for helping dogs behave a little better.

No More Distractions

Even dogs who have learned their lessons well— who heel nicely, come when you call, and go

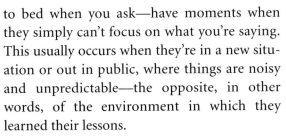

to bed when you ask—have moments when they simply can't focus on what you're saying. This usually occurs when they're in a new situation or out in public, where things are noisy and unpredictable—the opposite, in other words, of the environment in which they learned their lessons.

In real life, it's precisely in these unpredictable situations when good manners become so important. It's nice when your dog briskly comes running across the backyard when you call, but it's critical that he do the same when he's off the leash in a park or when his collar suddenly breaks on a busy sidewalk.

You can't anticipate everything that may happen, but you can look for situations that rattle your dog and break his concentration, and then look for ways to help him get used to them. Maybe your dog is skittish about traffic and street noises and gets so distracted or anxious that he ignores or doesn't notice your commands. Rather than avoiding these situations, seek them out, DeFranco says. With a lot of practice and a little bit of food, it's fairly easy to teach your dog to relax and stay focused in situations that used to scare him to death.

Here's how it works. Take your dog outside as you normally do. As soon as he encounters his first earful of noise, give him a small treat, DeFranco suggests. Give it to him right away, before he has a chance to get nervous. Keep looking for distractions—a noisy intersection, a crushing crowd of people, or whatever it is that makes him flighty or anxious—and reward him as soon as they occur.

Once he realizes that all those distracting sights and sounds signal treats, he'll focus less on what's going on around him and more on you—or at least on the good things he hopes you're holding in your hand.

HOT AND BOTHERED

Trainers often hear from owners who complain that their dogs are attentive and focused during their evening lessons, but then turn obstinate and cranky during the day. It's not their imaginations. In the summer, especially, dogs really may learn better in the evening or early in the morning, says Quenten London, a training consultant with the National Institute of Dog Training in Los Angeles. The reason why is not a big mystery. Here's how you can understand the classroom from your dog's point of view.

1. In July, go to the closet and put on the biggest, heaviest fur coat you own.

2. Go outside and practice some energetic heeling and sitting for 10 minutes.

3. Stagger inside, sponge off the sweat, and debate whether to call 911.

With their heavy fur coats and their relatively inefficient internal cooling systems, dogs are much more sensitive to heat than people are, London explains. During the warm months, even a few minutes of exercise or training can just about wear them out. This is why they usually learn best during the cooler times of day.

CHAPTER NINE

WHERE TO PRACTICE MANNERS

Where dogs learn makes a big difference in how well they learn.
Kitchens are nearly perfect, while yards are a little tricky. Choosing the
right place will make training quicker and easier for both of you.

Anyone who has ever bought real estate knows that the three most important things to consider are location, location, and location. Those who are teaching dogs, however, never hear much about location, and that's a mistake.

"It really is something that people need to take into consideration," says Barbara S. Simpson, D.V.M., Ph.D., diplomat for

The kitchen is a great place to train dogs. It has happy associations and tantalizing smells that concentrate their minds wonderfully.

the American College of Veterinary Behaviorists and adjunct assistant professor of veterinary medicine at North Carolina State College of Veterinary Medicine in Raleigh. Dogs are intensely aware of territory—areas where they live or visit often. When they learn new things, they associate those things with the places where they learned them, says Dr. Simpson.

People often discover this for themselves when their dogs return home after spending several weeks with a trainer. The trainer gives a glowing report and explains all the wonderful things the dogs have learned and how nicely they behave. So the owners give a few commands themselves—and their dogs just sit there. It may take a few weeks or even months for them to transfer those lessons to their new locations.

No Place like Home

Dogs do most of their learning at home. There are different rules in every part of the house. You may encourage your dog to sleep in the living room but not in the kitchen. A paw on the knee may be welcomed in the den but not in the dining room. Dogs learn most quickly when their lessons are tailored to and practiced in

different parts of the house, says Gillian Ridgeway, director of training for Who's Walking Who dog obedience center in Toronto. Here's what you can expect from each place.

The kitchen. The kitchen is an ideal spot to begin training, says Ridgeway. Dogs generally have good, cozy feelings about the kitchen, and that makes it a stress-free place to practice. And with the exception of families that include hungry teenagers, it's usually quiet and free from distractions.

"The best time to train a dog is when she's hungry," adds Ihor Basko, D.V.M., a veterinarian with practices in Honolulu and Kilauea, Hawaii. Dogs begin detecting food smells the instant they walk into the kitchen. They're going to be very motivated to learn what you have to teach—and even more motivated to get the reward that follows.

The living room. The living room is sort of an all-purpose training area. It's usually the biggest room in the house, which means there's plenty of room to practice commands such as "heel" and "come." It's also a good place to reinforce lessons learned in other parts of the house as well as to teach specific skills, like staying off the furniture, Ridgeway says.

The backyard. Only dogs who graduate magna cum laude from the indoor portion of their educations should attend graduate school in the yard. Otherwise, forget it. Yards are filled with intriguing smells, leaves to bark at, cats to chase, and a million other distractions. Whatever your dog has learned so far, putting it to work in the backyard is a tough test. It's here that you'll learn whether or not she's ready for the next big step.

POOCH ?!? PUZZLER

Why do dogs dig after pit stops?

Unlike cats, who thoroughly bury their waste, dogs usually just go and run. But sometimes, they complete their ablutions by giving the ground a few half-hearted digs. It looks as though they're imitating cats, and not doing a very good job of it.

Some experts believe that this pawing is a way for dogs to spread their personal scents, says Barbara S. Simpson, D.V.M., Ph.D., diplomat for the American College of Veterinary Behaviorists and adjunct assistant professor of veterinary medicine at the North Carolina State College of Veterinary Medicine in Raleigh. They don't actually scratch the waste, just the ground around it. Sebaceous glands between their toes leave an oily scent. Not every dog performs this ritual, Dr. Simpson adds. Dogs who are timid are reluctant to call attention to themselves. Dogs with dominant personalities, however, have a perpetual need to proclaim their superior status. Pawing the ground tells the world they were there.

The Real World

It's nice when dogs behave at home, but that's just the beginning. They also have to learn the ropes in the outside world. There's a lot of noise and confusion out there. They need to learn to listen and obey even when they're on crowded sidewalks or surrounded by traffic. "Dogs are very aware of home versus not home," Dr. Simpson says. "They will act very differently in unfamiliar locations."

Dogs who have made the grade in indoor training can graduate to the outdoors, where the distracting sights, smells, and sounds will really test their mettle.

It's in the real world that your dog will practice the most important skill of all. Veterinarians call this skill generalization. It's the ability to transfer all of her learnings from one environment to another.

Start with tennis lessons. Dogs who leave the familiar comforts of home sometimes feel like tourists in New York City: totally overwhelmed and distracted. They need a safe place to practice their initial out-and-about lessons. Dr. Simpson recommends tennis courts. "They're great places to do training," she says.

"They're out in the open with all the distractions, but they're still in confined areas."

You won't be practicing there long, she adds. Once dogs are past the initial rush of excitement, you can move to other venues to teach the basics. In the meantime, don't forget to pick up after your dog. "It's terrible to play tennis around piles of dog poop," Dr. Simpson says.

Go to a beer store. The next classroom is a lot more challenging than tennis courts because it's public, noisy, and packed with people. It's the parking lot at a beer store on a Saturday afternoon. "You have lots of foot traffic going in and out, but people are usually in a rush or have their hands full, so they don't stop too often to pet your dog," Ridgeway says.

It doesn't matter what lessons you're teaching, she adds. The point of training in a busy environment is that your dog will learn to pay attention to you no matter what else is going on. It's challenging. Any dog can learn "stay" in the living room when there's just the two of you and you're only standing a foot away. In a parking lot, there are tons of distractions, and you'll have room to move farther and farther away. This is an important part of training because it teaches your dog to watch you even when people come between the two of you.

There are limits to what dogs can learn at first in an environment like this, Ridgeway adds. During the first few tries, you'll probably lose your dog's attention as you step away. At that point, move closer or take your dog to a less distracting area. Too often, people don't do that.

"People tend to move farther away and insist that the dog do whatever they're telling her to do," Ridgeway says. "Don't stick to your guns on this." Training, she explains, always involves a few steps forward and an occasional step back. It's normal.

Go for a ride. Part of real-world training should also include riding in the car, says Dr. Basko. There's a pragmatic reason for this. Dogs who don't spend much time in cars tend to get sick on the upholstery. There's also a safety issue. Dogs have to go for rides sometimes, if only to go to the vet. They need to learn to stay in the backseat and not wedge themselves under the brake pedal.

Dr. Basko recommends periodically taking your dog's crate, cardboard box, or whatever she sleeps in and putting it in the backseat of the car. Put a few treats or toys in the crate and invite your dog in. Do it once a day. After awhile, you can forget the crate—your dog will naturally gravitate to the backseat. "Most dogs will learn this in a week, 2 weeks at most," says Dr. Basko.

SAVING FACE

Most people think of their dogs as somewhat short humans—until the dogs do something blatantly doggish, like shoving their noses in someone's privates. Dogs are always going to do embarrassing things, so it's worth having a few responses ready for those inevitable faux pas.

When Your Dog Does This...	Say This
Humps	"Sorry about that. He thought you were a flat tire."
Snacks from the litter box	"Did you know that's considered a breath freshener among dogs?"
Chases his tail	"He's been like that ever since we saw *Twister*."
Rolls in pond scum	"And to think that people pay big bucks for seaweed body wraps when they could have this for free."
Crotch-sniffs	"You could ask him to shake now, but you've already been introduced."
Jumps up	"Care to dance?"
Breaks wind	"He learned that from my husband."

PART THREE

MANNERS AT HOME

Human ways must seem mighty strange to dogs. We fill our houses
with furniture, then don't let them on it. We invite people over, but
object when dogs sniff their bottoms. We want them to be friendly,
but get annoyed when they follow us all around the house.
Despite some confusion, dogs can learn the basic manners they
need at home. Manners are necessary—not to spoil their fun,
but to help everyone get along a little better.

CHAPTER TEN

Respect for Possessions

pages 48–53

CHAPTER ELEVEN

Protecting Your Space

pages 54–59

CHAPTER TWELVE

Greeting Visitors

pages 60–65

CHAPTER THIRTEEN

Greeting the Mailman

pages 66–68

CHAPTER FOURTEEN

Mealtime Manners

pages 69–74

CHAPTER FIFTEEN

Bedtime Manners

pages 75–81

Special Skills

pages 82–87

Turn On the Light • Get My Slippers
• Excuse Me • Wipe Your Mouth
• Ring the Bell • Wave Bye-Bye

CHAPTER TEN

RESPECT FOR POSSESSIONS

Chew toys are dandy, but expensive leather is much more satisfying.
You can't reduce dogs' instinct to chew, but you can help them understand
that some things are always off-limits.

Everyone who lives with dogs has had the experience of discovering a soggy, chewed slipper on the living room floor or has watched with dismay as their dogs attempted to dig to China through the freshly shampooed carpet. Whether you have a puppy or an older dog, a certain amount of property destruction comes with the territory. It's what healthy, well-adjusted dogs sometimes do, says Sarah Wilson, a trainer in Gardiner, New York, and co-author of *Childproofing Your Dog.*

But there's a difference between occasional hijinks and systematic wreckage. Some dogs seem to have a natural tendency to destroy, and once they get started, it can be hard to make them stop. If you're going to preserve your possessions, you need to understand a little bit about how dogs think. Whether they've been chewing for years or are just getting started, you can teach them to show a little more respect—if not all the time, at least most of the time.

Five Types of Destruction

Every dog has different reasons for destroying possessions, but most of the reasons can be grouped into a few main categories, says Kimberly Barry, Ph.D., a certified applied animal behaviorist in Austin, Texas.

"I'm young and my teeth hurt." Puppies go through a teething stage from about 14 weeks to 6 months. Chewing on things helps ease the pain of sore gums, says Dr. Barry.

"I'm young and curious and I don't know any better." Just as children will pick up, poke, and dismantle things, young dogs take things apart with their mouths. In part, this is exploration. They're seeing what tastes good or has an appealing texture. But it's also inexperience. Puppies and young dogs naturally want to chew and don't yet understand that they're supposed to destroy their toys, not yours.

This Lhasa apso pup chews a lot, both out of curiosity and to help soothe the pain of teething. Chew toys will keep her jaws busy.

"It's fun." People often suspect that their dogs are chewing books, shoes, and furniture legs because they're angry or resentful about something. But their motivation is usually a lot simpler. Chewing feels good, and they like doing it, says Dr. Barry.

"I thought it was mine." By the time they're a year old, most dogs understand which objects they're supposed to play with and which they're supposed to leave alone. Unless, that is, no one took the time to teach them the difference. People often give dogs discarded shoes, baseballs, and other family items to play with. But dogs can't distinguish between a tennis shoe that they're allowed to chew and one that's supposed to be off-limits.

"I'm unhappy." The most destructive dogs of all are usually those who spend a lot of time alone and don't have a lot of excitement or stimulation in their lives. A bored dog will look for entertainment, and destroying the couch is certainly entertaining, says Dr. Barry. In addition, dogs need ways to relieve stress and anxiety, and an hour of shredding wallpaper helps them dispel bad feelings.

Giving Up Bad Habits

Chewing is a natural puppy stage, and it's almost impossible to make them stop, if only because their urges to chew can be a lot stronger than your desire to make them stop. Adult dogs who get destructive are harder to handle—not only because they're strong enough to do real damage very quickly but also because they become set in their ways, and habits are hard to change. "The problem with furniture ripping,

BREED SPECIFIC

The retriever breeds often destroy by chewing because they've been bred to work with their mouths. Dachshunds, beagles, and terriers such as Cairn terriers (right) tend to destroy by digging because they were bred to flush rabbits and other small game from their burrows.

linoleum pulling, wallpaper tearing, and chewing is that these activities are self-rewarding," says Wilson. Dogs like having fun, and destroying things, from their point of view, is a heck of a lot of fun. "It's not too hard to teach them not to do it while you're looking on, but most will continue to gleefully do it when they're alone," she says.

If you're willing to spend a little time teaching the basics, every dog can learn to control destructive impulses, Wilson adds. The only way to succeed, however, is to never let it happen. Just as an ex-smoker can't afford to take a single puff, a destructive dog has to go cold turkey. Three weeks of good behavior will be wiped out if he gets one afternoon of guilty pleasures. So you have to be vigilant. The idea is to make it impossible for dogs to indulge their destructive habits, while at the same time making destructive activities a little less pleasurable—and less necessary.

Out with the Bad

Regardless of why dogs chew, the one thing they have in common is that they don't understand that certain things in the house are completely and entirely yours, and that these things are not to be chewed, torn, scratched, or wrestled with. Even when they suspect that they're doing something wrong, they have a hard time linking specific actions, like eating the bedspread, with the displeasure that you show later on. That's why you have to catch them in the act. No one enjoys being on perpetual guard duty, but most dogs will start to get the idea within a few weeks—and the longer they go without destroying anything, the more the habit will start to fade.

Put temptation out of sight. The writer Oscar Wilde once said that he could resist everything except temptation. That's a sentiment that dogs can relate to. Since they aren't going to resist temptation on their own, you have to take temptation away from them. Before you go to bed, put shoes in the closet and close the door. Put stuffed animals out of reach. Keep expensive—and toothsome—valuables on higher shelves. The longer dogs are deprived of destructive opportunities, the less likely they'll be to resume the habit later on.

Keep them under wraps. You can't expect a dog to behave when you're not around, at least at first, Wilson says. You can't watch your dog every minute, but you can tuck him away in a safe place when you're occupied with other things, such as sleeping. Wilson recommends moving his bed into the laundry room or another comfortable place so that he won't get into mischief at night. Put him in the yard when

Dogs with destructive tendencies need to be supervised, but it's inconvenient to hold a leash all the time. This golden retriever has no choice but to stay put when her owner puts her foot on the leash.

you're cleaning the house or running errands. The idea isn't to banish him, but to make it impossible for him to destroy things when you're not around to catch him.

The one problem with this approach is that dogs crave human contact. Leaving them unsupervised and alone for more than about four hours will make them lonely and bored—and more likely to vent these feelings at the first opportunity. You'll have to plan on spending as much time with your dog as possible, Wilson says. Once he starts getting out of the destructive habit, you'll be able to relax a little more.

Use a leash indoors. It doesn't take long for dogs to get into trouble—2 or 3 minutes alone is plenty. "Sometimes, keeping them on leashes can help," says Inger Martens, a trainer and behaviorist in Beverly Hills, California. A quick tug when they start showing interest in something that they shouldn't is a great reminder, especially when a "No!" is thrown in. The leashes also allow you to keep them nearby and out of trouble.

It wouldn't be very comfortable to spend your days holding a leash, so you'll want to get creative, Martens says. When you're relaxing or reading, for example, put your foot on top of the loose end of the leash. Or thread the leash through a belt loop. At least you'll have your hands free while you do other things. And you won't have to do this indefinitely, Martens adds. Most dogs learn more quickly than people think they do, and a few weeks of close supervision is usually enough.

Cut them no slack. Dogs who get away with destructive behavior once are going to keep doing it. A half-hearted "no" or an angry look doesn't have a lot of impact, especially since the joys of destruction may outweigh the threat of a lukewarm reprimand. Take a stand and then follow up on it, Wilson says. When your dog starts chewing, scratching, or digging, immediately tell him "no." Make sure that he understands that you're not happy and aren't going to put up with it. Dogs respect authority and they want to please. When they understand absolutely and without confusion that you're

unhappy, they'll look for activities that you do approve of.

You can help them out by giving them an acceptable alternative, Wilson says. When you scold your dog and he stops what he's doing, quickly give him something else to play with. When he takes it, praise the heck out of him. This will help him make the obvious connection: "When I play with her things, she's unhappy. But when I play with my things, she's happy and gives me a tasty treat. I like this!"

Teach at the moment of destruction. Dogs have pretty hazy memories. Ten minutes after destroying a $100 pair of shoes, they won't even remember doing it. This is why it doesn't do any good to scold them or drag them to look at something after the fact. They may look guilty, but they're really just reacting to your mood—they won't have a clue what's going on,

A good way to stop dogs from chewing is to offer them something better, like a tennis ball.

says Rolan Tripp, D.V.M., a veterinarian in La Mirada, California, and affiliate professor of applied animal behavior at Colorado State University College of Veterinary Medicine and Biomedical Sciences in Fort Collins.

Also, yelling at them after the fact can make them nervous about your arrival, and that's the last thing you want. The only reprimand that works is one that's given right when they're in the act, Dr. Tripp says. If you miss the opportunity, about all you can do is take a deep breath, clean up the mess, and wait for the next time.

FAST FIX Some dogs are very selective about what they chew and will return to the same object again and again. A quick way to discourage them is to give the object a bad taste—by coating it with Grannick's Bitter Apple pet repellent, available in pet supply stores. Bitter Apple comes in a spray designed for plants, a generic spray, and a less acidic furniture cream. Another option is to coat objects with a diluted solution or paste containing alum, an extremely sour additive sometimes used to keep pickles crisp. "It's safe and it has a terrible taste," Wilson says.

In with the Good

Since dogs love to chew—and, in fact, they need to chew—it would be cruel to take away verboten objects without giving them some kind of alternative. Finding toys that dogs like can be a challenge because they generally prefer things that belong to their owners. A pair of shoes is redolent with your personal scent, and that makes dogs feel very satisfied as they

Hollow toys that can be loaded with tasty tidbits, such as Buster Cubes and treat balls, provide dogs with challenging alternatives to destructive behavior.

tear them apart. Socks, neckties, handbags—nothing is safe.

Every dog can be satisfied, however, if you shop around a bit. A lot of dogs adore tennis balls, for example, and will ignore everything else as long as one or two are lying around. Some dogs love stuffed toys, and others will happily work over rawhide bones. One toy that's worth trying is the Buster Cube, says Dr. Barry. This is a hollow toy that you fill with dry food. As your dog noses and bats it around, pieces of food will occasionally fall out, and this will hold almost any dog's interest.

No matter how much a dog loves a toy, however, he can't play with it all the time without getting bored. That's why experts recommend giving them a whole slew of toys—not all at once, but in rotation. Since dogs don't remember much from one day to the next, putting one toy away at night and giving them a "new" one in the morning makes every day seem like Christmas, says Dr. Barry.

The problem with toys, of course, is that they're not indestructible. Dogs have strong jaws and sharp teeth, and they're persistent. You're going to be buying a lot of toys. "When I give my dogs a fuzzy toy, I may as well hand them a $20 bill and let them chew that up," Wilson says. The ideal solution is to find a toy that your dog loves and that is also tough enough to withstand his attentions. Wilson recommends giving dogs chew toys called Nylabones, which are a lot tougher than balls or natural chews such as rawhide. Because they're made of synthetic material, however, Nylabones may not have the same attraction as your shoes. You can make them more tempting just by rubbing them between your hands. This will cover them with your scent. For most dogs, that makes toys worth chewing.

Dogs adore objects that carry their owners' scent, which is why they're so attracted to shoes. Adding your scent to your dog's toys by rubbing your hands on them will make them much more attractive.

CALL FOR HELP

Most dogs chew, dig, and destroy because they enjoy it. For some, however, it's really a cry for help because they can't bear to be alone.

Dogs traditionally lived in packs—tight-knit societies of dogs who slept together, played together, and ate together. Today, dogs consider people to be their packs, but the people are often gone for long periods of time. Some dogs get nearly frantic with loneliness, a condition called separation anxiety, says Kimberly Barry, Ph.D., a certified applied animal behaviorist in Austin, Texas.

Dogs with separation anxiety can be extraordinarily destructive, often destroying thousands of dollars worth of property and possessions. Dogs suffering from this condition aren't going to get better without some professional help, Dr. Barry says. Separation anxiety is easy to recognize, however. The signs include:

- The destruction occurs mainly when you're away from home—or at least, that's when it's most extensive.
- Your dog has hurt his mouth, cut his paws, or otherwise gotten injured while tearing things apart.
- He is most likely to damage objects when he's obviously upset or anxious.

CHAPTER ELEVEN

Protecting Your Space

Dogs always want to be close to their owners, which means they have a tendency to crowd their personal space. They need to learn that everyone has a zone of privacy that doesn't include them.

If you're ever in the mood to make someone really uncomfortable, stand about 3 feet away—then move closer. We don't consciously think about it, but we have an area of personal space that surrounds us. When people invade this space and come closer, we start feeling a little crowded and claustrophobic.

Dogs have a rule governing social distance, too. For the most part, it can be summarized as, "The closer, the better." This is why people sometimes find themselves competing for bed space with a canine comforter. Or struggling to breathe when a 75-pound retriever climbs in their laps. Or trying to get a moment's peace while a four-footed shadow follows them from room to room.

"Imagine if your spouse, let alone anyone else, came up to you 20 times a day, bumped you, and said, 'Honey, touch me,'" says Sarah Wilson, a trainer in Gardiner, New York, and co-author of *Childproofing Your Dog*. "After about an hour, you'd say, 'Hey, go get a life.'"

Gimme Some Lovin'

To understand why dogs are so clingy, it helps to know their evolutionary history. Dogs are very social animals who have always lived in packs,

Dogs always crave companionship. Even when they can't have their owners' undivided attention, they're happy just to be near them.

which are the equivalent of canine communes. Dogs in packs ate, slept, hunted, and played together. They were happy when they were with each other and lonely when they weren't.

Our dogs don't live in packs anymore, but they have retained their craving for companionship. Most dogs learn to adjust to human styles. They know that people leave for work in the morning, come back in the evening, and everything is fine. They understand that people do things that don't involve them, like washing dishes and reading books. They're more than willing to sleep on the floor, chew a toy, and otherwise entertain themselves until the people in their lives are ready to give them attention.

Then there are dogs who never give up. They act as though a minute of separation were a lifetime. They follow people around, nudge their hands, and generally make pests of themselves in their bids for attention.

"They're constantly checking in for reassurance," says Rolan Tripp, D.V.M., a veterinarian in La Mirada, California, and affiliate professor of applied animal behavior at Colorado State University College of Veterinary Medicine and Biomedical Sciences in Fort Collins.

A Shot of Confidence

Whether dogs are begging for reassurance or are merely fond of attention, clingy behavior gets exhausting after a while. To help dogs be less demanding and more secure, here's what experts recommend.

Reward seldom, but well. Dogs would make perfect salesmen because when one bid for attention doesn't work, they're always ready to trot out another one, knowing that their owners will eventually give in.

"When you reach out and pet your dog every time he approaches, he's going to think, 'Aha, she obeys my every command,'" Wilson says. The only way to stop the pester-and-reward pattern is not to give in. Ignore the hand nudges and leg leans. Wait for your dog to do something that really deserves praise, such as going upstairs when you tell him to. Then give him plenty of attention and make him feel good, Wilson advises.

Reward mindfully. A character in the "Peanuts" comic strip once said, "Happiness is a warm puppy." We tend to give our dogs a lot of attention even when we aren't thinking about it—by rubbing their ears as we read or absentmindedly petting them when they lean against us. This affectionate give-and-take is the reason that dogs and people love each other. But for

BREED SPECIFIC

Nearly every dog will occasionally crowd his owner, but dogs who were bred to work closely with people, such as retrievers, are known for making it their life's work. Dogs such as Akitas and Rottweilers, on the other hand, were bred to work on their own, and they tend to maintain more personal space.

"For many golden retrievers, personal space is about 3 inches," says Sarah Wilson, a trainer in Gardiner, New York, and co-author of *Childproofing Your Dog*. "For salukis [left], it can be as much as 8 feet."

dogs who are already clingy, it nearly makes them desperate to push farther into your space, says Wilson.

Dogs are pretty smart about what works and what doesn't. If you make a conscious effort to only give strokes occasionally and to ignore your dog the rest of the time, he will realize that his crowding behavior isn't paying off and will start to back off, probably within a few days, says Kimberly Barry, Ph.D., a certified applied animal behaviorist in Austin, Texas. In the meantime, get ready for an increase in attention seeking, she adds. Dogs who are used to endless attention won't give it up right away. In fact, they may be more nervous and in-

This corgi is learning that a little distance from his owners isn't a disaster as long as he can see them. When he's calm, he won't need the leash anymore.

secure until they get used to the change and realize that everything is still fine.

Drop your voice. Researchers have found that people customarily raise their voices when they talk to dogs, just as they use higher voices when talking with children. There's nothing wrong with this except when you're trying to discourage certain types of behavior. Dogs don't understand many words, but they do understand tone. You may be saying, "Silly dog, don't climb on me," but if your voice is cheerful and high, what your dog hears is "C'mon up!" explains Suzanne Hetts, Ph.D., a certified applied animal behaviorist in Littleton, Colorado.

Dogs are very responsive to low-pitched voices, probably because "top dogs" who are annoyed will respond with low growls or warning grumbles. When you want your dog to give you some space, tell him so in a tone that he will respond to—low and gruff. Use his name first to get his attention, then say "off" or "down," Dr. Hetts advises.

Keep them close—but not too close. Dogs always keep a close eye on their people, but for some dogs, just watching isn't enough. They stand up when their people stand up. They follow them from one room to another. They even push their way into the bathroom. The reason they act this way is that they can't bear to be alone for even a moment. You can help them be more confident by teaching them that the world doesn't end just because you're out of sight, says Dr. Tripp.

• Put your dog on a leash and tie the leash to something across the room from where you'll be sitting. He won't be able to

Why do dogs lick faces?

When two dogs meet, after they've gone through the sniffing preliminaries and are getting to be friends, one dog will invariably lick the other dog's face. They do the same thing with people—not just when they meet, but as a way of saying hi.

There's a reason for all this oral affection. In the days when dogs roamed wild, lower-ranking dogs in the pack would periodically lick the lead dog, says Kimberly Barry, Ph.D., a certified applied animal behaviorist in Austin, Texas. It was their way of conveying respect and affection.

A sloppy kiss isn't only about affection, however. Puppies quickly learn that they can get extra nourishment by licking their mother's face. Not only does this make her feel happy and more disposed to extend the dinner hour, but the puppies may get lucky enough to catch a stray bit of food from her last meal.

length of time that you're gone. You want to stay gone long enough that your dog notices, but not so long that he gets frantic.

- Dogs who are insecure don't get nervous only when their owners walk out the door or leave the room. They start getting anxious when they first detect the clues that a departure is imminent. As a final stage in the process, Dr. Tripp recommends helping your dog get used to all the signs and sounds that precede your departures. Pick up your keys, rattle them, and then put them down, he suggests. Do this periodically while you read a magazine or watch TV. Open and close the garage door a few times.

Rattling keys, opening and shutting doors, and other departure sounds don't faze this German shepherd. He has learned to stay calm when his owners are getting ready to leave.

come over and nudge you, but you'll still be in sight and close enough for him to stay calm. Do this several times a day until he starts to get used to the distance.

- Wait until your dog is relaxed and comfortable. Then get up and leave the room for a few seconds. He may look as though he's watching the Titanic depart, but he'll calm down quickly once you come back in and sit down again. Do this several times, keeping your absences very brief, Dr. Tripp advises. Over a period of days and weeks, gradually increase the

Dogs who take up a lot of space on the couch aren't just trying to get comfortable. They may be making a bid for "top dog" status in the household.

Your Space or Mine

Most dogs intrude on people's space because they're lonely or in need of reassurance. Some do it for the opposite reason: to put you off-balance. Dogs are very physical by nature, and they use physical contact not only to express affection but also to establish chains of command. A dog who shoves, hip slams, or leans against other dogs—or people—is establishing a position of authority. A dog who shoves past your legs when you open the door or who takes up increasing amounts of space on the couch by leaning against you is essentially saying that he's taking over, Wilson says.

Dogs give a similar message when they defend their food bowls or grumble when someone tries to move them off the couch. They're taking it upon themselves to claim their space and whatever (and whoever) happens to be in it. This type of attitude invariably gets more pronounced over time, which is why trainers recommend stopping it quickly.

"Your dog should know that everything in his world is yours, but that you are nice enough to share," Wilson says.

Give your dog a job. In the world of dogs, every dog occupies a certain place on the social ladder—top dogs, bottom dogs, and dogs in

Put on your jacket and take it off. The idea is to do all of these things so often that your dog begins to learn that these and other "leaving signals" don't mean much of anything. Then, when you really are leaving, he'll be less likely to work himself into a lather beforehand—and he'll be less likely to latch on to you when you're home as well.

• As long as your dog is sitting or lying quietly, walk over periodically and give him a reward—something to eat or just some attention, Dr. Tripp says. The idea is to reward him for not being nervous. What you don't want to do is reassure him when he's acting nervous. Giving dogs attention when they're frightened reinforces the emotion and will make them even more nervous, he explains.

If you keep doing this for a few weeks, your dog will come to understand that he actually does pretty well when you're not around—and, more important, that you'll always come back.

between. The same thing occurs in human families. Problems occur when dogs think that they're higher on that ladder than you. The best way to turn their thinking around is to make them understand that nothing in life is free and that all good things come from you. No matter what they want—their supper, a walk outside, or the biscuit you're holding in your hand—they should expect to work for it, says Dr. Tripp.

Have your dog sit before you put down his food. Require him to lie down before you open the door. Don't give him attention when he comes to you—he should wait until you offer it. The idea isn't to be a tyrant, but to make sure that your dog understands who is calling the shots. Once he understands that, he'll be much less likely to make demanding incursions on your personal space, says Dr. Tripp.

Mean what you say. It's human nature to be circumspect, out of politeness, if nothing else. But when dogs are pushing into your space, it's time to take a stand. Make a few basic rules and then follow through—not occasionally, but all the time. Suppose you've decided to keep your dog off the couch. Well, keep him off. Cut him no slack. No matter how cute he looks when he's sneaking up, tell him "off." Make sure that everyone else in the family does the same. For dogs no less than people, firm convictions and the willingness to follow through create respect, and even dominant dogs don't crowd the people they respect.

Show him the floor. Another way to protect personal space is to insist that dogs sleep on the floor and not on the bed. Some dogs view beds and other furniture as being status symbols as much as creature comforts.

"If your dog is making moves on your space, you don't want to confuse him by making him an equal at night," Wilson says.

FAST FIX Probably the easiest way to reclaim your personal space is to make your dog's spot of choice—on the couch, for example—unusable, says Dr. Tripp. Put a footstool where he sits. Cover that side of the couch with an uncomfortable sheet of plastic. Or keep a pile of books there. Once your dog loses access to his throne, he'll be less likely to lord it over you in other ways, he explains.

This kelpie-Labrador mix is learning that he must sit quietly and not push his way past his owner when she opens the door.

CHAPTER TWELVE

GREETING VISITORS

Dogs have their own ways of saying hi to each other. But their customary greetings to people need a little work. Most folks take a dim view of four-legged cannonballs with inquisitive noses.

Imagine a world in which dogs were the ones wearing suits, living in houses, and having dinner parties to meet the neighbors. Visitors arriving for a Sunday soirée wouldn't be greeted with handshakes or hugs. They'd get jumped on. They'd feel cold noses pressing into private places. They and their hosts would turn in circles and sniff each other's tails.

It's not our way of greeting visitors, but dogs have been doing it forever, and it works just fine. "All the usual greeting problems that people encounter are perfectly normal ways that dogs greet other dogs," says Brian Kilcommons, a trainer and behavioral expert in Gardiner, New York, and co-author of *Good Owners, Great Dogs*.

Dogs are a lot more physical than people. Puppies greet their mothers by jumping up and licking their faces. It's a gesture

This Lhasa apso jumps up to get closer to her owner's face. Jumping up is natural dog behavior, but unless they're discouraged from doing it at a young age, it can quickly get out of hand.

that means, "I'm glad you're my mom, and I'll always do what you say." Adult dogs also greet each other face-to-face, followed by a face-to-rear follow-up. It's their way of introducing themselves and determining who has the stronger, more dominant personality.

What works among dogs, however, is uncomfortable, impertinent, or rude when people enter the picture. No one looks forward to being on the receiving end of a probing nose or watching in dismay as their dogs leave muddy paw prints on their visitors' pants and jackets.

Jumping Up

It's cute when a puppy who weighs just a few pounds and barely reaches your ankle jumps up on her hind legs and reaches up with her paws. But that cute little puppy grows fast—some dogs put on 100 pounds in 6 months—and her cute little jumping won't be charming for long.

Dogs have a natural tendency to go airborne, says Wayne Hunthausen, D.V.M., a veterinarian in Westwood, Kansas, and co-author of *Handbook of Behavior Problems in Cats and Dogs.* For one thing, it's their way of greeting other dogs. More important, we inadvertently teach our dogs to do it, either by ignoring or encouraging it when they're young or by merely sighing and standing back when they do it later on.

"If you have people coming in and saying, 'Oh, it's okay, I don't mind it when your dog jumps up,' she's going to think it's fine to keep doing it—and she's going to jump on the next poor soul who shows up at your door," says Kilcommons. Dogs aren't always quick learners, he explains, and it's difficult for them to understand that while it may be acceptable to jump on one person, it's wrong to do it to someone else.

It's easy to teach puppies not to jump, but older dogs take more work because jumping is a habit and jumping is fun. "For some dogs, jumping up is more fun than eating," Dr. Hunthausen says.

Teach him with bribes. "Try walking in the door with a piece of food at nose-level," says Dr. Hunthausen. "Use a favorite food that smells great, and tell your dog to sit." You have to move quickly because you don't want your dog to have time to make her usual moves. As long as she sits and doesn't jump—and if she truly likes the food you're holding, she's going to do what you say—give her the snack. Then turn around and walk out the door. Come right back in and do the whole thing again.

Dogs are very good at linking actions with rewards, especially when the reward is food, Dr. Hunthausen explains. It won't be long before

PUPPY DOG TALES

Doggy Maître D'

At the Lake Sonoma Winery in Geyserville, California, the breads, cheeses, and wines are perfectly matched; there's a stunning view of the valley; and the service is tail-wagging friendly. Thunder, a 7-year-old Labrador–Great Dane mix, comes to the office every day with his owner, winery operations manager George Christie. Thunder meets arriving visitors at their cars and escorts them to their tables. Should someone drop a napkin or a purse, Thunder is right there, ready to pick it up and return it.

After 3 years of greeting up to 200 guests each day, Thunder has a lot of fans, Christie says. "People come back looking for Thunder, and they send us notes about him."

Thunder's manners are impeccable, but they aren't perfect, Christie adds. At 125 pounds, Thunder is very fond of food and has been known to cast a covetous eye at the guests' dinner plates. It's not that Thunder begs, Christie says. It's just that everyone enjoys feeding him.

your dog thinks to herself, "She walks in the door, I sit down, she gives me food. Cool!"

Admire the ceiling. "When your dog jumps on you, ignore it. Cross your arms and look at the ceiling," says Sarah Wilson, a trainer in Gardiner, New York, and co-author of *Childproofing Your Dog.* A jump is a dog's way of asking for attention, she explains. When she doesn't get what she's asking for, she'll start looking for something that works better.

Reward downward mobility. Physical techniques like giving your jumping dog a knee in the chest will certainly get his attention, but they're not as effective as other, gentler methods. Rather than criticizing bad behavior, trainers

TEACHING "OFF"

Every dog who aspires to social fitness needs to understand the word "off." This simple command can be used to keep dogs off doors, couches, and counters as well as off guests. It's an easy command to teach, and it works a lot better than opening the door and silently praying that your dog will stay down for a change.

Here are two ways to teach it.

1 When you're expecting company, put a leash on your dog and let it dangle behind her. When guests arrive and she jumps up to greet them, step on the leash. She won't achieve the height she's looking for, and her forward momentum will pull on her collar. In essence, she'll be correcting herself. When she quits jumping, praise her for being so smart and obedient.

2 Put a leash on your dog and hold the free end. When she jumps up to greet guests, firmly tell her, "Off!" and snap the leash to one side. A dog who is jumping is on two legs, which means her balance is off. Pulling the leash sideways will force your dog to put her feet back on the ground. Once she's down and relaxed, if only briefly, praise her for being so good.

say, it's more effective to reward good behavior. So ignore the jumping and praise your dog lavishly when she's sitting calmly or otherwise staying earthbound, Wilson says.

Of course, some dogs jump so often that it's hard to find an opportunity to praise them. The only way they're going to earn your praise is if you help them disrupt their usual habit. Carry a whistle and give a shrill blast as soon as your dog's front feet start to leave the ground, recommends Dr. Hunthausen. The noise will startle her, and she'll pause to think things over. That's precisely when you want to pet and praise her, he explains.

FAST FIX The next time you're expecting company, arm yourself beforehand with a spray bottle filled with a vinegar-and-water solution, mixed half-and-

Dogs who have been spritzed once or twice with a vinegar-water solution while jumping up tend to remember. Just showing them the bottle will remind them to keep their feet on the ground the next time company is over.

half. When your dog goes up for her usual greeting, spritz the solution in her mouth, says Julia Jones, an instructor and Northwest region program manager with Canine Companions for Independence in Santa Rosa, California. The solution is harmless, but it tastes yucky. "When your dog sits down to think about what just happened, praise and pet her," she says.

Rude Sniffing

It looks (and feels) strange to us, but there's a perfectly good reason that dogs stick their noses between people's legs or into their bottoms: communication. Unlike people, who depend mainly on senses such as speech and sight, dogs use smells to talk to each other. Their sense of smell is about 100 times more sensitive than ours, which means that they collect information that we don't even know exists. And private places, both in people and other dogs, are rich repositories of informative scents.

It's difficult to teach dogs not to sniff people—it's just what they do. What you can do, however, is make other, less invasive types of greetings even more interesting and rewarding for them. When people come over, for example, immediately tell your dog to sit and give her something to eat, says Dr. Hunthausen. "You want her to learn that sitting gets a better payoff than a nose full of a stranger's aroma."

As a last resort, you may want to try a more aggressive tactic. Some trainers recommend keeping an air horn (the kind used on a boat) near the front door. Encourage guests to give a blast when your dog starts her routine. Dogs are accustomed to people putting up with their sniffing, so they always act surprised when someone responds negatively, says Judith Halliburton, a trainer and behaviorist in Albuquerque, New Mexico, and author of *Raising Rover*. Their usual reaction is likely to be, "Whoa, I've never had that happen before," and then they'll walk away. If they get the same reaction every time they try their sniff-and-greet routine, they'll start looking for other ways to introduce themselves, she explains.

I Pee Because I Love You

It's hard for people to relate to, but many dogs will urinate as a way of saying hi. In their world, a little splash of urine is the ultimate form of respect, a gesture that means they respect your authority, Kilcommons explains. That's why it doesn't help to scold them for doing it. They've just made a profound expression of submission, and they'll be crushed if you're unhappy and reject them. In fact, they will feel more submissive than before—and may urinate a little more.

"The more excited your dog gets, the less attention you should give her," Kilcommons says. Keeping greetings calm and low-key helps dogs stay calmer, and they're less likely to urinate when they're relaxed and secure. "When guests come over, ask them to not focus on your dog or lean over to touch her," he adds.

It's also possible to teach dogs to use drier greetings when people come in the door, Kilcommons says. Put a box of treats by the front door. When people come over—or when you come home yourself—take a treat and im-mediately toss it on the floor before your dog has a chance to urinate. Then, walk on past and let your dog concentrate on finding and devouring the snack. "If your dog does the drill enough times, she'll learn to look for the treat rather than put on a show for your visitor," explains Kilcommons.

A Little Help from Your Friends

One reason that greeting problems are so hard to stop is that they occur at precisely those times when you don't want to think about training. It's hard to give your guests your full attention, for example, when you're opening the door with one hand and wrestling with your dog with the other.

Trainers agree that the only way your dog will quit jumping on, sniffing, or otherwise annoying visitors is if you stop her the minute she does it—and that may require keeping your guests waiting at the door for a minute or two. No matter how embarrassing it feels, it's probably not as bad as you think. After all, there are millions of dogs in this country. There's a very good chance that the people you're welcoming have dogs of their own. They'll understand exactly what you're trying to do.

One way to help people understand what you're trying to accomplish is to put a small sign on the front door, something like "Puppy training in progress. Please be prepared for anything!" Visitors will know beforehand what you're up to, and you won't feel as though you have to pretend that everything is fine when, for example, you open the door with one hand and haul back on your dog with the other.

STRANGE behavior

Name MAGGIE

Breed LABRADOR RETRIEVER

Age 8

The Behavior

Maggie is an old dowager of a dog with affection and good humor to spare. But she has an unfortunate habit. When people sit down, Maggie stealthily tries to slip all of her 78 pounds into their laps. And because Maggie loves everyone, no one escapes—not the visiting members of the Republican committee, deacons of the church, or her owner's 80-year-old mother-in-law, who barely weighs as much as Maggie. Her owner doesn't want to put her in a crate, but she doesn't know how else to control Maggie's relentless lap patrol.

The Solution

Maybe no one is admitting it, but someone is making Maggie feel really good about sitting on laps, says Brian Kilcommons, a trainer and behavioral expert in Gardiner, New York, and co-author of *Good Owners, Great Dogs*. Dogs love to be loved, and somewhere along the line, Maggie learned that laps are a great place to get all the love, hugs, and kisses that she ever wanted.

Guests are in a difficult situation when their host's dog insinuates her way into their laps, he adds. No one wants to be rude and take the chance of insulting the host. Even people who aren't very fond of dogs probably feel compelled to give her at least a little attention—and that's all the encouragement Maggie needs. It also seems likely that Maggie is a crowd-pleasing type who thrives on the cries of "Oh, Maggie" that her stunt provokes.

There are two things that Maggie's owner will have to do to teach her that lap scaling is not an acceptable sport. First, the family should hold a meeting in which each member swears to uphold the group's decision to not encourage Maggie—thus discouraging the one person (or more) who is secretly encouraging her and undermining the efforts of the rest.

Second, everyone has to vow to be vigilant in the presence of guests and quickly slip Maggie a little something as soon as she makes her move. "When she goes to sit in someone's lap, they should have her sit or lie down," says Kilcommons. "Then reward her for it. Give her a treat. Tell her what a good girl she is, and cheer and laugh while she's on the floor—instead of when she's sitting where she's not welcome."

CHAPTER THIRTEEN

GREETING THE MAILMAN

Mailmen spend a lot of their careers braving barking dogs. It shouldn't be part of their job, but it's an unfortunate reality. Dogs, on the other hand, see *their* job as protecting their territory. Reconciling these conflicting agendas can be a challenge.

For Molly, a 10-year-old Labrador retriever in Philadelphia, it's the best time of day. At 11:15 every morning, the hair on the back of her neck rises, her ears prick up and rotate forward, her tail starts swishing, and she lets loose with a cacophony of barks loud enough to be heard three doors down.

It's the mailman, same as yesterday. All he has in mind is dropping a few letters through the slot, but Molly sees things differently: He's a trespasser who, if he knows what's good for him, will get off her porch. Which he does, of course. At which point, Molly, feeling excited but self-assured, settles down for a rest. It's a stressful moment in her day—and in the mailman's—but tomorrow they'll do it all again.

Who Can Argue with Success?

Nearly every dog gets worked up when the mailman comes to the door. Partly, it's just excitement. "They think, 'There's someone out there, and I want to go, too,'" says Wayne Hunthausen, D.V.M., a veterinarian in Westwood, Kansas, and co-author of *Handbook of Behavior Problems in Cats and Dogs.*

More important, dogs want to protect their territory. They don't understand that strangers come into people's lives every day. They've been bred for thousands of years to be protective and loyal to their owners. In their minds, anyone who hasn't been personally introduced is a potential threat, and they're not about to sit back without kicking up a fuss.

Doberman pinschers have been bred as guard dogs, so they're more likely to bark at strangers than other breeds. They can learn to be quiet, but they rarely relax entirely.

Even though the arrival of the mailman is a daily event, dogs bark and carry on as though every visit is the first one. The reason for this, says Dr. Hunthausen, is that they're always successful. The mailman approaches, they bark, and he leaves—and dogs congratulate themselves for doing such a good job. And with every repetition, they get even more deeply rooted in their habits.

"If dogs were human, they'd all be in therapy because they'd be compulsive hand washers or chain-smokers," says Judith Halliburton, a trainer and behaviorist in Albuquerque, New Mexico, and author of *Raising Rover*. "Dogs are absolutely habit-driven, and the more they replay a reaction, the more ingrained it becomes."

If you don't have neighbors nearby, and if your mailman isn't the nervous type and the front door is more or less indestructible, this routine may not be a problem. But the furious barking, if it's loud enough and lasts long enough, can drive almost anyone crazy. Especially because it happens every single day—except, of course, on Sunday.

Restoring Quiet

It's never easy to teach dogs to greet mailmen graciously. For one thing, a lot of people work, so they aren't there to shush their dogs up. In addition, dogs have been barking at intruders for thousands of years, and they're unlikely to just give it up.

"Dogs with long-held habits need some kind of correction or distraction to get them off automatic pilot," says Dr. Hunthausen. "You have to do something to disrupt their pattern."

BREED SPECIFIC

Nearly all dogs bark when they hear someone approaching the house, but Doberman pinschers, German shepherds, and Rottweilers are among the loudest and most persistent because they've been bred to guard and protect their people.

- Pet supply stores and catalogs sell a product called the Super Barker Breaker. It's a relatively simple device with a sensor and an amplifier. When dogs bark, the machine barks back, loudly and at a high pitch that dogs dislike.

- Veterinarians sometimes recommend fitting dogs with special collars that emit bursts of citronella mist when they bark. Citronella is a natural substance that has a citrusy scent. Dogs dislike the smell, and the *pssst* sound of the mist distracts them from barking. Eventually, they figure out that it's their barking that causes that awful smell and noise, says Dr. Hunthausen.

- If you decide to get really serious, you may want to invest in a Scraminal detector. A hand-size motion detector available in pet supply stores, it makes a high-pitched beep when dogs get too close to windows or doors, which means they can't see the mailman arrive or leave.

- The lowest-tech strategy—and in some ways one of the most effective—is to drop a few pennies in an empty soda can and tape the opening closed. When your dog starts barking at the mailman, toss the can in his general direction while telling him, "Quiet!" says Dr. Hunthausen. At the very least, the clattering sound

will make him stop barking momentarily. If you do it often enough, your dog will perhaps be less likely to start barking in the first place.

Silence Ahead

Since dogs are creatures of habit, it's a lot easier to work with them before they discover how much fun it is to bark. "Prevention is the key to getting them to not go ballistic when they see the mailman," says Dr. Hunthausen. Here are a few ways to ensure that your mailman always gets a first-class reception.

Block the view. Many mailmen are just as quiet as dogs are noisy, which means the only way your dog knows the mail is coming may be when he sees the mailman coming up the walk. Pulling the blinds when you leave for work— or rearranging bookcases or other pieces of furniture so it's harder for your dog to see out windows—may be enough to keep him from getting started, says Dr. Hunthausen.

Increase their confidence. Dogs have a natural urge to protect their property, but they're also social animals who welcome friends. You can teach them to think of the mailman as a friend, says Dr. Hunthausen. He recommends staying home with your dog for a couple of days. "The minute your dog spies the mailman, tell him to sit and give him a reward," he says. Most dogs are more interested in eating food than in barking at the mailman. Once they get in the habit of sitting quietly—and eating— when someone approaches the door, they'll be more likely to be blasé about the arrival of unexpected visitors even when they're alone, Dr. Hunthausen explains.

Dogs can't eat and bark at the same time, as this German shepherd can attest. If you're home when the mailman arrives, give your dog a treat to keep his mind off the "intruder."

Keeping the Edge

One reason that mailmen have such a hard time of it is that many people are reluctant to curtail their dogs' protective urges. This shouldn't be an issue, Halliburton says. Dogs can be great watchdogs even when they know enough to be silent when the mail arrives.

"Dogs usually know the difference between a regular visitor and a threatening one," she explains. "You don't need your dog to defend your house against the mailman and the paperboy. Correcting him when he does that will make him more discriminating, but it won't diminish his instinct to protect."

CHAPTER FOURTEEN

MEALTIME MANNERS

Eating is one of life's great pleasures, and dogs make the most of it. But sometimes, their appetites lead them to unauthorized dining, such as stealing or mooching. That's when it's time to tame their appetites and teach them some etiquette.

Sometimes fate throws a dog a tempting morsel that can't be resisted. Take chicken breasts topped with ham and Swiss cheese, lined up neatly on the kitchen counter, with no sentry in sight. It was too much for Francine, a portly yellow Labrador, who managed to scarf down three of the four uncooked cordon bleus while her owner, John Murphy of Fort Worth, Texas, was busy answering the phone. Francine then walked to the back door, raced a few times around the yard, and vomited.

So much for social graces. In no more than 15 minutes, she committed the sins of grand theft poultry, gluttony, and unsightly purging. Worst of all, she wouldn't think twice about doing the same thing again if she got the chance.

Dogs and people have entirely different notions of etiquette, especially at mealtimes. People view eating as a social affair, and consideration for others is a high priority. But among dogs, getting as much as possible is on page one of the dining guide. They think that it's perfectly reasonable to be shameless beggars who steal food off the table, eat way more than their share, and spill a lot on the floor in the process,

says Judith Halliburton, a trainer and behaviorist in Albuquerque, New Mexico, and author of *Raising Rover*.

More Than a Meal

Your dog's manners, or lack of them, made sense in the evolutionary scheme of things. Dogs were hunters and scavengers who depended on their strength and resourcefulness to stay well-fed. Their first rule was, "If you can get it, it's yours." The second rule was, "Eat up because you may not get more anytime soon."

BREED SPECIFIC

Labradors aren't any more likely to raid the trash than other breeds, but they often get blamed anyway because they look as though they're guilty. Along with dachshunds, basset hounds (left), and beagles, Labradors have slow metabolisms that make them gain weight even when they haven't been foraging.

Nutrition aside, dogs make several assumptions about food that people don't share.

Food is scarce. Even though dogs today don't have to worry about where their next meal is coming from, they share the attitudes of their feral ancestors and cousins, who typically ate only once every two to three days. Naturally, they stuffed themselves silly whenever they had the chance.

Food is power. Dogs used to live in highly organized groups called packs. Within a pack, every dog had a social rank and knew who was above her and who was below her in status and power, says Nicholas Dodman, professor of behavioral pharmacology and director of the Animal Behavior Clinic at Tufts University School of Veterinary Medicine in North Grafton, Massachusetts, and author of *Dogs Behaving Badly*. When the pack made a kill, the dogs ate in order of rank. Your dog may not seem to care or even be aware of her place in the family, but on some level, power is very much on her mind.

Dogs have only been domesticated for about 10,000 years or so. Eventually, they may lose some of their old attitudes and start thinking about food more in the way that people do. But in the meantime, dogs will be dogs, and good manners are not going to come naturally. They have to be taught, coerced, or tricked to eat like civilized members of the family. How you approach the problem depends on your dog's personality and what, exactly, she's doing wrong.

Begging

In their perpetual quest for food, many dogs become accomplished beggars, and few people can enjoy a meal under their soulful, apparently starving gazes. No matter that your dog is 10 pounds overweight and ate an hour ago—she has your number. She knows that when she cocks her head, lowers her nose, raises her eyes—or whatever her usual tricks are—you're going to give in to guilt and fork something over.

Begging is a common mealtime faux pas, and it's one of the easiest to correct. Dogs tend to do things that work. When they've begged at the table and been rewarded, they're going to keep doing it, says Julia Jones, a service-dog instructor and Northwest region program manager for Canine Companions for Independence in Santa Rosa, California. On the other hand, when they realize that their old tricks don't work, they gradually give them up. Here's a three-part strategy that experts recommend.

1. "Only feed your dog out of her own dish," Jones says. Dogs go where the food is.

Dogs get emotional about food because it symbolizes power and status. This 5-year-old vizsla is getting ready to assert his authority by moving in.

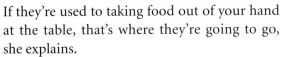

If they're used to taking food out of your hand at the table, that's where they're going to go, she explains.

Some foods are meant to be given by hand, of course. It's fine to give your dog biscuits and other finger foods. But don't hand them over when you're in the kitchen or anywhere else where begging has been a problem, Jones says.

2. Only give them dog food. There's nothing unhealthy about giving dogs small amounts of human food, and any sensible dog prefers a juicy scrap of steak to a bowlful of dry kibble. Once your dog gets a taste for the good stuff off your plate, she'll be very reluctant to walk away empty-handed.

3. Don't give in to guilt, and don't hesitate to walk away. "You have to ignore the stares," says Halliburton. "As long as you pay attention to her when she's begging, she's going to hold out hope that you'll give in. But once there's no acknowledgment that she is even there, she'll know that she's just wasting her time."

Thieving

Some do it in plain sight. Others wait until their owners are out of the room or asleep. Then they make their moves. A ham-and-cheese sandwich on the counter disappears. The trash is tipped over and thoroughly sifted. A child is distracted for a moment—and her ice cream cone is gone.

If dogs sat on juries in criminal courts, charges of food stealing would never get a conviction because every dog steals food on occasion and some do it all the time. It all goes back to their days in the wild, when sneaky dogs tended to be long-lived dogs.

CALL FOR HELP

It's not unheard of for dogs to break into their food bags and gobble 5 to 10 pounds of food in just a few minutes. Or they will raid the counter and devour an entire ham. Beyond the obvious problem of thoroughly bad manners, this type of eating can trigger bloat, a life-threatening condition in which the stomach fills with gas, often within an hour.

Dogs with bloat will have an obviously swollen abdomen that is as taut as a balloon. They'll also be uncomfortable and may pace, breathe heavily, or try without success to vomit. Most common in large, deep-chested dogs such as German shepherds, Great Danes, and Doberman pinschers, bloat is always an emergency, and you'll need to get your dog to a veterinarian right away, says Wayne Hunthausen, D.V.M., a veterinarian in Westwood, Kansas, and co-author of *Handbook of Behavior Problems in Cats and Dogs*.

Training books invariably recommend "correcting" dogs when you catch them in acts of thievery. It's true that dogs want to please their owners, and a few disapproving "no's" may convince them to be more upstanding canine citizens. But food is a very powerful reward, whether it's given freely or pilfered, Halliburton says. "Lots of times, you can teach dogs not to steal food when you're standing there, but they'll go back to it when you turn your back."

Rather than depending on formal training to stop food stealing, many trainers prefer to use sneakier approaches. The idea isn't necessarily to convince dogs to do the right thing, but to make the act of stealing less rewarding.

Make the counters uncomfortable. When asked why he robbed banks, the notorious criminal Willie Sutton explained that that's where the money is. Dogs recognize this logic. They grab food from counters because that's where food usually is.

Since you can't guard the counters and their contents all the time, trainers have devised some ingenious ways to discourage unauthorized forays. Halliburton recommends buying a roll of two-sided carpet tape and putting a strip all along the edge of the counters. Then put some bait—a fresh piece of bread, for example—a few inches behind the tape. Carpet tape is tremendously sticky. When your dog jumps up and reaches for the bait, the tape will grab her probing paws and maybe pull out a few hairs. Dogs hate sticky sensations, Halliburton explains. If you do this for a few weeks, your dog may come to loathe the whole idea of counters and stay away entirely.

Bait the trash. From a dog's point of view, a trash can is like an all-night diner. It's always open, it's easy to get to, and it's full of wonderful rotten odors. Short of stashing the trash behind closed doors or buying an expensive can with a tight-fitting lid, the easiest way to keep dogs out of the trash is to make it an upsetting place to visit. Pet supply stores sell spring-loaded, mousetrap-like devices with large paddles that make a loud pop when they're jiggled. You can put them on top of the can or inside, on top of the trash.

"When your dog gets into the trash, the trap is going to pop, and she'll think the trash did it," Halliburton explains. "She'll think twice before she does it again, though it will probably take a few lessons."

Rattle their nerves. Dogs dislike loud, clattery noises. You can take advantage of this aversion to keep them off counters or away from the trash can. Jones recommends threading a string through the center of a hot dog and tying several empty soda cans to the other end. When your dog takes the wiener and runs, the resulting clatter will startle the heck out of her. Putting a few coins in the cans will make the clattering even worse. "This works especially well with dogs who are wise to the idea that they can get away with stuff when they're alone," says Jones.

Scraps of food sprinkled with hot-pepper sauce and dropped into the trash can will put a stop to dogs' trash-raiding tendencies.

FAST FIX A quick way to take the fun out of stealing is to season a few scraps of food with hot-pepper sauce or ground red pepper. You can put the food on the counter, in the trash, or wherever it is that your dog usually makes her raids.

The extra-hot sensation won't hurt her, but it will offend her tastebuds. Some dogs soon decide that human food is too spicy for their tastes and will stop their foraging, Jones says.

Gorging

Like people, dogs overindulge in foods that taste great. Unlike people, they think that just about every food tastes great. "Overeating is just sheer dog," says Wayne Hunthausen, D.V.M., a veterinarian in Westwood, Kansas, and co-author of *Handbook of Behavior Problems in Cats and Dogs.* "Many dogs don't start to feel satiated until they've gone miles beyond meeting their caloric needs."

This tendency to gluttony means that many dogs are perpetual moochers as well as overweight. And because their digestive systems can't always keep up, dogs who stuff themselves have a way of getting sick afterward—usually behind the back door or on your best carpet.

Since gluttony is part of a dog's evolutionary package, there's not much hope of teaching restraint. According to Dr. Hunthausen, you can slow her down so at least she doesn't get sick.

• Giving dogs more dietary fiber will help them feel full even when they eat a little less. Either use a high-fiber food, available from veterinarians and pet supply stores, or supplement their diets with such things as cooked oatmeal or lightly steamed vegetables.

• Giving dogs several small meals a day instead of one big meal is another way of helping them feel more satisfied. They'll still wolf down their portions, but at least they won't get indigestion afterward.

This golden retriever is eating at a sensible pace because the tennis ball in her bowl prevents her from gobbling.

• Veterinarians sometimes suggest putting a tennis ball or some other large object in the food bowl. This forces dogs to pick around the object and eat more slowly.

Guarding

Mealtime etiquette takes a dive when dogs feel as though they have to protect their food or even the empty dish. They don't do it because they're bad-tempered, Halliburton explains. They do it because their ancestors did it and because it's their way of reinforcing their status in the family pack. It's no big deal when a dog growls at another dog who's showing too much interest in her food. But dogs who get testy toward people are forgetting the rules—that the humans, not the dogs, are the leaders and they have the right to go anywhere they want, including near the food bowl.

Food aggression can be a problem because it invariably leads to other kinds of aggression. To

help your dog feel more relaxed and less defensive, here are a few tips you may want to try.

Feed the people first. From their days in packs, dogs understand that those who eat first are the leaders and aren't to be trifled with. This is why trainers recommend that the people in the family eat before the dogs do—and in a place where the dogs can see them. "This is a simple step, but it can make a big difference," says Sarah Wilson, a trainer in Gardiner, New York, and co-author of *Childproofing Your Dog.*

Watch him eat. "When you feed your dog, don't leave the room," says Halliburton. "She doesn't need privacy, and if you put her food down and hit the road, she may think that it's because she's entitled to have the room to herself while she eats."

Don't give food for free. A subtle way to teach dogs to be less aggressive about food is to remind them that they wouldn't be eating at

One way to curb food aggression is to reinforce your leadership by watching your dog eat her meals.

all if it weren't for you. "Make your dog do something for you before you do anything for her," says Wilson. Tell her to sit or to lie down before you put the dish down. If she doesn't do what you ask, put the dish out of sight. Then try again in a few minutes. Hunger will eventually prevail, and your dog will have a clearer understanding of the chain of command in the family, Wilson explains.

FAST FIX On those occasions when your dog is properly polite when you approach her food, drop a special treat into the dish, Wilson suggests. Not only will this reward her for being good but also she'll realize that good things happen when you're near her bowl, she says.

Being first in line at the supper table is a sign of status among dogs. This terrier mix doesn't like waiting her turn, but she's learning that people have higher status than she does—and that it doesn't pay to get pushy about food.

BEDTIME MANNERS

Considering how much dogs like to sleep, it's surprising how disruptive they can be at night. Here are a few tricks to ensure that bedtime is the peaceful time that it should be.

Sleeping is something that dogs do very well. They drop off with a speed that would make a trucker jealous. "Most dogs sleep more than half their day away, and some sleep much more," says Kathleen Murnan, D.V.M., a veterinarian in Bedford, Texas. "And most dogs go right to bed when their owners turn out the lights at night."

Dogs rarely get insomnia, in other words. When they do, it's usually because they're not feeling well or they have to go outside to water the lawn. But despite this gift for slumber, nights in some houses resonate with noisy sighs, perpetual pacing, and the click-clicking of hard little claws on hardwood floors.

Some dogs need less sleep than others, which means they spend some of their nights looking for things to do. Others feel that it's their job to act as security guards and pace through the house every few hours. Still others accumulate so much energy during the day that they simply can't fall asleep at night. Regardless of the reason, most of these dogs are perfectly happy staying awake at night. Their owners, who may spend hours with pillows clamped over their heads, have a different opinion.

All-Night Dogs

Since the vast majority of dogs sleep so well—at night, in the afternoon, and any other time they lie down—people are always surprised when they discover that they have a night owl in the family. While some dogs have internal clocks that are naturally a little skewed, most nighttime perambulations occur when dogs aren't doing a whole lot during the day. The combination of boredom and stockpiled energy almost guarantees that they'll do some pacing, tossing, and turning.

Since their insomnia invariably becomes your insomnia, you'll want to put some effort into tuckering them out before they hit the hay, says Marty Becker, D.V.M., a veterinarian in Bonners Ferry, Idaho, and co-author of *Chicken Soup for the Pet Lover's Soul.*

This Norwegian elkhound puppy is just doing what comes naturally. It's common for dogs to sleep 14 hours a day or more.

Dogs who lie around all day tend to be wakeful at night. This bull terrier mix is burning off energy and will be knocked out by bedtime.

Walk their little paws off. It was only in the past generation or so that dogs made the transition from the barnyard to the backyard. Before that, dogs were expected to work—as herders, hunting companions, and trackers. Dogs who were active all day didn't have much energy left at night, says Dr. Becker.

Modern dogs have a very different lifestyle. They spend as much as 80 percent of their time alone, and they pass the time by sleeping. Dogs who sleep all day long are not going to need as much sleep at night. More important, dogs have evolved as physically active animals. Those who sleep all day accumulate vast amounts of energy. The only way to burn it off is get them moving, preferably a lot. Nearly every dog needs a minimum of 20 minutes of exercise twice a day, once in the morning and again in the evening, says Dr. Murnan. Some very energetic breeds, such as Labradors and Border collies, may need two or three times this amount, especially when they're young.

Since a dog's every instinct tells her to move, this isn't something you'll have to struggle with. Throwing a ball—or a rawhide, stick, or whatever it is your dog loves—around the yard for a half-hour will burn off a lot of energy. Walking is great exercise, and running is even better—not only because it helps blow off steam but also because it gets the two of you out of the house and into new worlds of sights and sounds. Mental stimulation as well as physical exercise almost guarantees that a dog will sleep soundly, says Dr. Becker.

CALL FOR HELP

It's rare for dogs to suffer from full-blown insomnia. However, older dogs may develop the canine equivalent of Alzheimer's disease. Called cognitive dysfunction, this condition can make dogs extremely restless as well as confused. Since insomnia is one of the first signs, you should call your veterinarian if your dog's usual sleeping habits take a sudden turn for the worse. There isn't a cure for cognitive dysfunction, but there are a number of medications that can help relieve the symptoms.

Teach them to play alone. Unlike cats, who have evolved as solitary animals and will happily play by themselves, dogs spent their evolutionary history in tight social groups called packs. Dogs in packs did everything together. Our dogs don't live in packs anymore, a change they haven't quite adjusted to. That's why suburban dogs with vast, fenced yards don't run around any more than their apartment-dwelling cousins. Unless someone is out there playing with them, they just sleep by the back door and wait for you to come outside.

Dogs may be reluctant to play alone, but they're perfectly happy to eat alone. Experts have found that it's possible to stimulate the former by forking over the latter. A toy called a Buster Cube, available in pet supply stores, uses food as a way to keep dogs entertained even when they're alone. This pushable toy has an inner compartment that holds bits of dry kibble. Dogs can smell the food inside, so they shove the toy around, releasing an occasional trickle of food. They eat the food, then shove the cube around some more. A fully loaded Buster Cube can keep them busy for hours, says Betty Fisher, a trainer based in San Diego and co-author of *So Your Dog's Not Lassie.*

Move back the dinner hour. Even dogs who sleep well at night may wake up early because their stomachs are growling—and dogs who want their breakfasts aren't about to amuse themselves while you sleep. Giving in to early-morning whines and nose nudges is a real mistake because dogs learn from success, says Dr. Murnan. What you can do, however, is feed them later in the evening, she suggests. Dogs with full stomachs are sleepy dogs.

Swap play for sleep. If your dog has been in the habit of waking you up early, Dr. Murnan suggests keeping something special—a rawhide or a favorite toy, for example—on the nightstand. When your canine alarm clock comes cruising, groggily hand over the treat. As long as it's interesting enough to occupy her for a half-hour or so, you'll buy a little extra snooze time.

FAST FIX Research has shown that supplements containing melatonin or chamomile can help people sleep, and they appear to work for dogs, as well, says Beth Brown, D.V.M., a veterinarian in Bradenton, Florida. Every dog will need a different amount, so ask your vet for advice.

A Place to Call Their Own

For more than 10,000 years, dogs have been bred to be companions for people. As a result, they depend on people's company and attention to be happy, says Dr. Becker. Many dogs, in fact, won't sleep well unless they're near—or even in bed with—their people. This is fine as long as you don't mind listening

It's hard for dogs to sleep soundly when they're uncomfortable. A basket makes a snug bed for these two Maltese to share.

With their thick coats and wild backgrounds, dogs can make themselves comfortable in places where people can't. A carpeted floor is better than anything their ancestors had, but it's not ideal, if only because dogs have an instinctive need to dig into something soft and make themselves a cozy burrow. Pet supply stores sell a variety of well-stuffed beds, including beds filled with fragrant cedar chips, which most dogs love.

But you don't have to spend money. A thick blanket folded into a square and put in a shallow cardboard box makes a great dog bed. Dogs who are comfortable are much less likely to get up and pace around, says Dr. Becker.

Surround her with your scent. Just as people sleep better when they're in their own beds or wrapped around their favorite pillows, dogs sleep best when they're surrounded with familiar scents. For dogs, nothing is more comforting than the scents of their owners.

"Take the blanket you're giving your dog and sleep on it for one night," says Dr. Becker. "Your smell on it will comfort her when she's trying to sleep alone."

Make a sleeping den. Dogs invariably gravitate toward small, enclosed places—the very end of the couch near the armrest, for example, or in a tight spot in a corner. Once again, this instinct has its origins in their ancient pasts, when dogs kept themselves warm and safe from predators in cozy little dens. It's easy to make a den at home, and it doesn't have to be anything fancy, says Dr. Becker.

• If your dog's bed or blanket is in the middle of the room, move it to a corner—in the bedroom, living room, or wherever you want

Dogs instinctively prefer enclosed areas to sleep in. This kelpie mix's bed, in a corner and hemmed in by sofas, creates a secure, denlike environment.

to doggy snores and you're willing to share a double bed with a canine comforter. But this much closeness isn't always appreciated. Reconciling these different agendas—the human desire for a good night's sleep and the dog desire for closeness—sometimes requires creative solutions.

Provide the bed of her dreams. Dogs enjoy their creature comforts. When they don't have a soft, special place to sleep, they generally look around until they find one—and their pacing and complaining can be mighty hard to sleep through.

her to sleep, says Dr. Becker. Simply being "protected" on two sides makes dogs feel safer and more relaxed, he explains.

• Regardless of where your dog sleeps, you can make things cozier by rearranging the furniture a bit so that it creates an enclosed space that's large enough for her to sleep in easily, but not so large that it feels wide open. Small areas hold heat, and your dog will enjoy the added comfort.

• Many veterinarians recommend using crates to keep dogs comfortable and secure. Crates provide perfect enclosed spaces that dogs like, and they're convenient for people because they're easy to move and clean. Older dogs don't always take to crates, however, so it's best to begin while they're young. Once they're used to them, most dogs will automatically walk into their crates whenever they want a little rest.

Crates aren't cages. They're safe and cozy dens where dogs enjoy spending time even when they're not sleeping.

POOCH PUZZLER

Do dogs dream?

Dogs fall asleep in an instant, and judging from their kicks and yelps, there's a lot going on in the land of Nod. "If you've ever watched your dog sleep and seen her twitching and wriggling around, you've probably seen her dreaming," says Charles McPhee, director of the sleep apnea patient treatment program at the Sleep Disorders Center of Santa Barbara, California.

No one is sure what dogs dream about. Maybe they're chasing rabbits, herding sheep, or wandering in a canine paradise where dog biscuits grow on trees. Regardless of what dogs dream about, experts believe that their dreams are probably ripe with the scents of adventure. Unlike people, who depend on sight and have mainly visual dream images, dogs smell the world before they look, listen, taste, and touch it. A large percentage of their brains is dedicated to scent, so it's likely that smell is the foremost experience in doggy dreams.

Rumbles and Roars

If you have a Boston terrier, a pug, or a boxer, you've probably discovered that "quiet" and "sleep" don't always go together. These dogs sleep just fine. But along with other short-faced breeds, they have unusually narrow airways. They've essentially been bred to be persistent, sonorous snoring machines, says Dr. Murnan. They snore so loudly, in fact, that people in separate rooms can hear the rumbles, even with the doors closed. "If you have one of these breeds,

Dogs with short noses, such as Boston terriers and bulldogs, are among the loudest snorers because their airways are uncommonly narrow. They wheeze and snort, as well.

about all you can do is wear earplugs," Dr. Murnan says. "There's just nothing you can do to prevent it."

There are ways to reduce if not eliminate snoring in other breeds, she adds.

Keep their weight down. Dogs who are heavier than they should be accumulate fatty tissue around their necks and within their airways. As the air passages become narrower, they act almost like wind instruments, causing noisy snoring.

Ask your veterinarian about allergies. Even minor allergies—to pollen, fleas, or anything else—can cause tissues in the airways to swell. This, in addition to an increased production of mucus, causes congestion that leads to snoring. You can often treat allergies at home, either by keeping your dog away from whatever it is she's sensitive to or by giving an antihistamine such as diphenhydramine (Benadryl). Your veterinarian can tell you the precise dose you'll need to give.

Most allergies are easy enough to treat, but figuring out what is triggering them is a daunting task. Seasonal allergies are usually caused by mold or pollen, but food allergies or allergic reactions to carpet fibers or household chemicals can occur year-round. If your veterinarian can't figure out what the source of the snoring is, he may recommend that you take your dog to a specialist for a full-fledged allergy screening.

FAST FIX Just as people snore less when they flip from their backs to their stomachs, dogs also get a little quieter when you roll them over, says Dr. Becker. It won't solve the problem, but it will help you sleep a little better—until she rolls over again.

Dogs often snore when they sleep on their backs. Sleeping on their sides, like this kelpie is doing, usually reduces the noise.

STRANGE behavior

Name RUSS

Breed BOXER

Age 2

The Behavior

Russ is a big, fun-loving dog who relishes time with his family. He loves them so much, in fact, that one day he decided he wasn't going to go to bed anymore. When he hears the familiar command "go to bed," he stares at his owners as though they're speaking a foreign language. When someone gets impatient and tries to lead him by the collar, Russ rolls over on his back and lies there like a sack of potatoes. Sometimes, people resort to carrying him to his bed in the kitchen, but their backs can't take it anymore.

The Solution

Boxers are known for being fun-loving, childlike dogs— and like most children, they don't like going to bed when their parents are still up and having fun, says Marty Becker, D.V.M., a veterinarian in Bonners Ferry, Idaho, and co-author of *Chicken Soup for the Pet Lover's Soul*. "The secret to solving Russ's problem is to make bedtime a good time."

Russ's bed should be his cocoon, a special place where he likes to spend time, Dr. Becker says. It needs to be clean and comfortable, for starters. It would also help if there was always a toy waiting for him when he went to bed— a new one every week. The bed itself may be part of the problem. Even if it's fluffy, well-padded, and thoroughly imbued with Russ's personal scent, he may not be entirely comfortable with the size. People like big beds, but dogs don't. Dogs like beds that are just big enough for them to stretch out— anything more makes them feel out of sorts.

Surroundings are also important, says Dr. Becker. Maybe the dishwasher makes a terrible racket. Maybe his bed is too far from the people's bedrooms. Maybe he just doesn't like being in the kitchen. Moving the bed to another room or another spot in the kitchen may make it more attractive.

It's also possible, says Dr. Becker, that Russ's bedtime routine is just too boring. He recommends spicing things up a bit—by taking Russ for a walk just before he goes to bed, for example. Or they could lure him to bed by holding something tasty in front of his nose and leading the way. Dogs almost always follow their noses, and bed will seem like an attractive place when there's food waiting.

TURN ON THE LIGHT

Fumbling for the light switch can be a real pain, especially when you have to navigate a maze of couches, chairs, and bookcases to get there. Dogs have a natural advantage because they can find their way in the dark better than people can. Problem is, most people don't take the time to show them how to do it. If your dog is tall enough to reach the light switch, he can learn to turn it on and off—especially if it's a push-button switch rather than the up-and-down kind.

1 Stand near a wall, pat it, and encourage your dog to jump up and put his paws against the wall. When he does, slip him a biscuit for his efforts.

2 Once he has practiced a bit and is comfortable balancing against the wall, start patting the switch with one hand and guiding his foot to the switch with the other. When he turns it on, say, "Get the light!" and give him something to eat.

☆ SPECIAL SKILLS ☆

GET MY SLIPPERS

It's no fun getting out of bed on a February morning and walking on a frigid floor while you search for your slippers. Why not ask your dog for help? Any dog can learn to fetch slippers, and retrievers have a special knack for it. Be sure to start with an old pair because dogs don't always want to give them back at first.

1 Start by teaching your dog the word "slipper." Toss one of your slippers a few feet away and say, "Get my slipper." Eventually, he'll grab it and bring it over. Trade him the slipper for a biscuit.

2 Once he knows what slippers are, hide them in an easy place, like behind an open door or under the bed, and encourage him to find them and bring them over. Once he has this figured out, you'll never have frozen feet again.

83

EXCUSE ME

Dogs always crowd the door, either because they're excited or because they really think it matters that they get through first. To prevent traffic jams, it's worth teaching your dog to politely step back so people can go through first.

1 When your dog is crowding the door, don't open it. First, use your leg to block him, and urge him back, saying, "Excuse me."

2 As soon as he backs away a couple of steps, tell him how smart he is. Then open the door and walk through, letting him follow. As long as he stays behind you, praise him and reward him for his patience. If he tries to muscle in ahead of you, keep the treat and keep practicing.

☆   S P E C I A L   S K I L L S   ☆

WIPE YOUR MOUTH

Dogs have lousy table manners. They put their whole heads in their bowls, swallow without chewing, and get food all over their faces. Every dog should know how to use a napkin to wipe his mouth when he's done.

1 Put a little food in your dog's dish—enough to get his interest, but not enough to dull his appetite for goodies. While he's eating, wrap a really good treat, like a piece of hot dog, in a towel.

When he is done eating and walks away from the dish, hold out the towel and say, "Wipe your mouth." As he sniffs around the towel for the hot dog, he'll wipe his mouth, more or less by accident. That's when you praise him and give him the treat.

2 With enough practice, your dog will understand that "Wipe your mouth" means he should rub his face on the towel. Hang the towel in a conspicuous place near his food dish. Even without the treat, he'll go to the towel and give his face a wipe.

RING THE BELL

Some dogs are too polite to bark or make a fuss when they need to go outside, which means you're always guessing. To clear up the confusion, you can teach them to ring a bell whenever they want to go outside.

1 Hang a string of bells near the door where your dog usually goes out. (Leather straps with jingle bells are available just about anywhere during the holiday season.) Rub one or two of the bells with a piece of hot dog.

2 Ask your dog, "Do you want to go out?" and invite him to sniff the bells. Once he smells "eau de hot dog," he'll take a lick—and the bells will ring. Quickly open the door, let him out, praise him, and give him the hot dog. While he's learning, stock up on hot dog bits. Let him out and reward him every time he rings the bells.

WAVE BYE-BYE

This trick gives dogs something to do with their hands, so to speak. Instead of trying to push through the door when guests depart, they can offer a proper salute. Waving bye-bye is easiest for short dogs with low centers of gravity, because they're better able to maintain their balance while sitting up.

1 Teach your dog to sit up by holding a treat over his head. When he reaches up for it while keeping his hind end on the ground, give him the treat.

2 Once your dog is comfortable sitting up, reach out your hand as though to shake his paw. When he reaches his paw toward your hand, pull back, tell him, "Good wave!" and give him a reward. Every time you practice, raise your hand a little higher when reaching out. This will cause him to wave higher.

PART FOUR

THE WELL-TRAVELED DOG

All dogs travel a little, if only to the vet for their annual checkups. But their traveling needn't end there. Dogs who behave well in all sorts of situations—in the car, at other people's houses, in hotels, and in wilderness areas—get invited on all sorts of outings. And every dog appreciates that.

CHAPTER SIXTEEN

DRIVING IN COMFORT

Car travel is a breeze for some dogs and a bitter pill for others.
Driving shouldn't be scary and it shouldn't make dogs sick. Here are a few
ways to help dogs adjust to life on the road.

All dogs go riding in the car occasionally, and most of them love it—sometimes a little too much, in fact. It's a lot of fun taking dogs places, but not when they stand with their feet on top of the front seat and bark all the way.

Then there are those who loathe car trips. They're afraid or they get carsick. They fidget, cry, and drool, sometimes for 10 hours or more. More than a few drivers have secretly wished they could put their dogs in the trunk along with the luggage in order to get a little peace.

Every dog, whether he's a seasoned traveler or a novice, can learn to be a better car companion, says Chris Walkowicz, a judge for the American Kennel Club, author of *The Perfect Match: A Dog Buyer's Guide*, and a frequent traveler who has logged thousands of miles with her various canine companions. Once dogs get comfortable and understand the etiquette, they'll enjoy—or at least rest easily for—every mile.

Making Good Memories

Dogs can't imagine the future, but they do remember the past. And for most dogs, past experiences in the car haven't always been pleasant—starting with that first trip when they left their litter mates. "The first ride in the car takes them away from the only family they've ever known," says Steve Dale, a radio host at WGN in Chicago, a syndicated columnist, and author of the book *Doggone Chicago*. "It can be heartbreaking."

Most dogs love going for rides, but even those who don't can learn to accept it and be more comfortable.

It doesn't get a whole lot better after that. Before dogs are 6 months old, they've taken several trips to the vet for examinations and shots. They may have gotten carsick a few times, and they've certainly gotten scared. And no matter how much reassurance their people give them, nothing changes the fact that they're riding in a machine that their ancestors never encountered.

People often forget how strange cars must seem to dogs, who can't really understand what they're all about. This is why veterinarians recommend taking the time to show dogs that cars are happy, exciting places. It doesn't happen overnight, but with a process called desensitization, dogs lose their fear and begin looking forward to life on four wheels.

- Since dogs like food better than just about anything, Dale recommends putting your dog's food bowl in the backseat or, if he's too scared even to climb inside, right next to the car. Feed him there every day for a week, he suggests.

- Several times a day, use the car in ways your dog can understand—by flipping treats onto the seats and encouraging him to go after them, or just by playing in the general area. "He should learn that good things in life happen when he's near the car," says Dale.

- Once your dog is comfortable in and around the car, slip into the front seat one day while he's eating in the back. You don't have to go anywhere. Let him get used to being in the backseat while you're in the front. Do this a few times, then actually start the car. Let the motor run for a minute, then shut it off. Do this three or four times a day for a few days.

- By this time, your dog will think that the car is a pretty cool place to hang out. So it's time

A full food bowl makes dogs very happy. This golden retriever is learning to associate the car with the thing he loves best.

to take a drive, maybe just to the end of the driveway and back. "If your dog whines or paces or shows other signs of stress, you may be moving too fast for him," says Dale.

- Every day or so after this, take your dog for a drive, gradually increasing the length of time you spend in the car. "Go somewhere you know your dog will enjoy," Dale says. "Get him french fries at the nearest fast-food restaurant. If you make every car trip upbeat and positive, your dog will learn to love the car. This process seems to take forever, but it does work."

Cruising in Comfort

Dogs get bored during long trips just as children do. And in fact, bored dogs act a lot like bored children—whining, pacing, and making a fuss. Of course, most dogs who have decent manners at home will have decent manners in the car as well. Those who don't may need extra help.

"I teach my dogs a vague kind of command, 'settle,' which means, 'You can pick where you lie down, but settle down,'" says Gina Spadafori, pet-care columnist for Universal Press Syndicate and author of the book *Dogs for Dummies*. It's an easy command to teach, she says, although you'll probably want to pick the place you want your dog to lie down, at least at first. Take your dog by the collar, say "Settle," lead him to the spot where you want him to lie down, and tell him "Settle" again. Then tell him "Good dog," and maybe give him a treat. Obviously, you need to teach the basics at home

Dogs who roam in the car are always a nuisance. Their wandering is dangerous, too. A useful command for them to know is "settle," which means "Find a comfortable spot to lie down—then stay there." It's also a helpful command to use at home.

before setting off on your trip, she adds. Most dogs pick it up quickly, sometimes in as little as a few days.

Home Away from Home

The main reason that dogs get uncomfortable on car trips is that they're in a new environment and they're feeling insecure, says Darlene Arden, author of *The Irrepressible Toy Dog*. Reassurance doesn't help; it can actually make them more insecure because they think, "Wow, she's nervous too, so I guess there really is something wrong."

The easiest way to help dogs relax is to keep them in a crate in the car, Arden says. Dogs in the wild always lived in dens, and dogs today still prefer small, enclosed places. Crates smell

A crate in the back of the car provides a cozy, denlike environment and helps keep dogs safe.

like home and give comfort in the strange environment of a car.

They also provide protection, Dale adds. "The little guys can get bounced around really good in the car."

Carriers come in wire, soft-sided, and hard-plastic models. It doesn't matter what kind you buy, although soft-sided crates are easier to store when they're not in use. Dogs who use crates when they travel often sleep in them at home, so they're really very handy, Arden says.

Puppies take to crates right away, but older dogs are often a little reluctant to use them— and you don't want to wait until you're pulling out of the driveway to discover that your dog is going to howl nonstop unless you open the crate door. If he isn't used to a crate and you're planning a trip, see chapter twenty for advice on helping him make the transition.

An alternative to a crate is a doggy seat belt. This helps keep your dog safe, of course, but it also keeps him in one place. This can make a difference on long trips because a cold, probing nose is distracting. And more than a few dogs have decided to find a new place to sleep—like under the brake pedal. "My sheltie, Andy, uses a seat belt, and he can either sit or stretch out," Spadafori says.

Another option is to set up a barrier that divides the people part of the car from the dog part. Pet supply stores sell a variety of dividers, from netting material and nylon screens to metal wire grills. "Barriers give dogs a bit more freedom and space of their own to move around in, and they work really well," says Spadafori.

A special dog harness that attaches to the regular seat belt keeps dogs safe and secure while traveling.

When you're traveling, let your dog out of the car every time you take a break. This will give him a comfort stop and a chance to have a sniff around.

Rest Stops

When a dog's gotta go, he's gotta go—and the jiggling of the car and the small bladder capacity of the average dog means you'll probably be stopping a lot more than you'd probably like. You can't fight nature, but you can help dogs be better car partners by making nature's call a little less urgent.

Give them a break when you take a break. Even if your dog is happily sleeping in the backseat, rouse him whenever you stop the car, says Spadafori. If you don't, he's sure to decide he has to go as soon as you've settled back into your driving.

"Generally speaking, as often as you need to take a break, so will your dog," she says. Dogs younger than 8 months usually need a pit stop about every 1½ to 2 hours. Older dogs can usually last 3 to 4 hours.

Make every stop count. Dogs get a real kick out of watering grass, trees, and highway signs—not because they're desperate to empty their bladders, but because they're leaving their calling cards for other dogs. If you pack your dog back in the car as soon as he anoints a roadside bush, you can be sure he'll shortly be whining because he needs some real relief. Dogs aren't going to change their habits just because they're on the road, but you can make trips go more smoothly by following what some people call the three-bush rule: Dogs aren't done until they've squatted or lifted their legs at least three times.

Remind them what they're there for. Thousands of dogs stop at highway rest stops every year. That means there are thousands of smells to distract your dog from the business at hand. To ensure he doesn't get so distracted that he neglects to do his business, it helps if he understands a command that means "go," says Spadafori.

Every time your dog squats or lifts a leg, give a command like "hurry up" or "potty." Use the same command every time, and try to use it every time he relieves himself. Then praise the dickens out of him by saying "good hurry up" or "good potty." Eventually, he will link the command with the action and be more than happy to oblige, Spadafori says.

Roadside Dining

One of the joys of traveling is sampling new foods along the way. At least, that's the human perspective. Dogs feel a little different. For all of their enthusiasm about exploring new places, they're distinctly conservative about what they eat. Buying whatever types of dog food you can find along the way isn't going to make your dog—or at least his digestive tract—happy. And no one has a good time when you're stopping every five miles because your dog has diarrhea or is throwing up on the backseat.

Since you may not be able to find your dog's usual food when you're in different parts of the country, Spadafori recommends packing food from home and giving it to him at the same times that he usually eats.

Water is less of an issue. Even though streams at rest stops may be contaminated, most traveler's diarrhea is caused by the stress of the trip and not by something your dog drank. Still, you'll probably want to pack water because

dogs get hot when they're traveling and will probably need to drink more often than you'll want to stop.

Walkowicz recommends filling a plastic bag with ice cubes and putting it in a cooler. When your dog is looking thirsty, let him lick the ice. It's a lot easier than filling a water bowl and watching the water slosh all over the floor mats. Some people get a little fancier and use water bottles that are made especially for pets. These work best for small dogs—large dogs tend to pull the tops off and make a mess, Walkowicz adds.

Calming Upset Tummies

Dogs who aren't accustomed to car trips usually reveal their inexperience by getting carsick, sometimes before you've gotten out of town. Their stomachs usually get a lot sturdier by the time they're 9 months to 1 year old. But the excitement and stress of traveling, along with the rocking motion of the car, can cause nausea even in the most seasoned travelers, says Joanne Howl, D.V.M., a veterinarian in West River, Maryland.

Start on an empty stomach. Even though you want to keep your dog on his regular eating schedule, plan your trip so he hasn't stuffed himself just before you leave. "Give him a tiny portion an hour before you leave, just to settle his stomach," Dale says. "Then you can give tidbits spaced out during the trip that add up to the total meal."

Offer something sweet. "Give your dog a little bit of sugar on the ends of your fingers," suggests Walkowicz. "The sweetness seems to settle the stomach."

Peppermint is an old folk remedy for nausea, and it appears to work as well for dogs as it does for people. People who travel a lot with their dogs sometimes slip them peppermint candies every two to three hours.

Prevent nausea with ginger. Another time-tested remedy for carsickness is ginger, either in cookie or supplement form. People who take their dogs to shows and log thousands of miles a year use ginger all the time, mainly in the form of gingersnaps, says Walkowicz. If you want to give ginger supplements to your dog, use the human dose as a guide. For example, a

CALL FOR HELP

Cars trap enormous amounts of heat. When they're parked, the temperature inside can soar to 125°F in just a few minutes. This is uncomfortable for people, but it can be life-threatening for dogs because their internal coolers aren't very efficient. When they get too hot, they can suffer from heatstroke, a serious condition in which organs in the body essentially shut down.

Dogs with heatstroke will usually have bright red gums, glazed eyes, and very thick saliva. They will also pant heavily and may try to vomit.

Heatstroke is always an emergency that must be treated by a veterinarian. If you can't get to a veterinarian immediately, try to cool your dog quickly by soaking him with water, applying wet towels to his body, or by giving him ice cubes to lick.

50-pound dog should get about half of the human dose 1 hour before the trip.

Give them Dramamine. This over-the-counter remedy isn't as strong as some prescription medications, but it still may be helpful for preventing nausea. Veterinarians usually recommend giving 1 to 2 milligrams for every pound of weight, about an hour before traveling. Every dog is different, so you should talk to your veterinarian before giving it at home. Dramamine (dimenhydrinate) is better at preventing nausea than stopping it, however, so if your dog is already sick, it probably won't help much.

Dramamine is safe, but don't give it to dogs who have glaucoma or bladder problems unless you check with your veterinarian first.

Change the view. "Some dogs get sick in cars but not in vans," Walkowicz says. The reason for this is that the sight of scenery whizzing by can cause nausea even in regular travelers. She recommends keeping dogs in crates and turning them so the openings face away from the windows.

FAST FIX Driving with the car windows open gives dogs a blast of fresh air. Fresh air helps settle the stomach, and the windy sensation helps calm the part of the brain that causes vomiting, says Dr. Howl.

Travel Gear

People embarking on road trips always pack extra gear, such as maps, extra sunglasses, and good things to eat. The well-traveled dog needs to accessorize as well. Here are some essentials.

• Dogs who stick their heads out the windows need eye protection, such as sunglasses or goggles, available in pet supply stores. Even if you keep the windows closed, shades provide good protection from ultraviolet light and will prevent their eyes from getting irritated.

• Sunshine inside the car can get pretty intense, so you and your dog will want to wear a sunscreen with a sun protection factor (SPF) of

15 or higher. Dogs with thin fur and white faces have the highest risk of getting sunburn. Be sure to buy a sunscreen that doesn't contain PABA (para-aminobenzoic acid) or zinc oxide, which can be harmful when dogs lick them off.

• You can buy seat covers and hatchback liners at pet supply stores. They come in colors and styles to fit every vehicle, and they'll protect your car from the inevitable doggy accidents.

• Travel is never risk-free, so you'll want to take along a first-aid kit, just in case. You can buy kits at pet supply stores, and they usually contain such things as tape, bandages, a thermometer, and over-the-counter medications like Kaopectate and Pepto-Bismol.

• Cars are usually pretty warm, so dogs need more water than usual. Take along a gallon of spring water, or fill a bottle with tap water. You'll also want to have a weighted water dish, which will be less likely to tip than a regular bowl. Some people travel with collapsible bowls, which are easy to store when not in use.

You need to plan when taking dogs on long trips. Taking a few travel accessories will make the ride more comfortable for all the family.

STRANGE behavior

Name LADY

Breed PEKINGESE

Age 6

The Behavior

Lady is lovable and cuddly—and larcenous. For some reason, she is always stealing stuffed animals from the toy box and stashing them behind the couch. She isn't sneaky about it, either. She walks to the box, takes out a stuffed rabbit or seal, carries it through the bedroom and across the living room, then delicately deposits it between the couch and the wall. Lady's owners were charmed by this quirky behavior at first. Now they're not so sure, because her crimes are escalating. Lady has started boosting all sorts of soft things, including clothes, dish towels, and slippers. It's one thing when the grandchildren can't find a particular stuffed toy. It's another altogether when Lady's owners can't get dressed because their socks are missing.

The Solution

Appearances notwithstanding, Lady isn't in love with socks or stuffed animals, says Sarah Wilson, a trainer in Gardiner, New York, and co-author of *Childproofing Your Dog*. She's in love with attention. She probably picked up the first stuffed duck or bear because it felt nice to carry around. When she heard her owners say things like, "Would you look at that?" or "Isn't she cute?" she knew she was onto something big.

"Pekingese grasp concepts very easily," Wilson says. "They're quick to recognize a good gimmick. Lady's owners made a fuss over her for playing with stuffed animals, and she has just played it to the hilt."

Lady isn't going to change without help—the rewards have been too good. "If Lady doesn't get a response when she takes things, it won't be long before she decides that it's not worth it," says Wilson. This will require a little bit of fortitude on her owners' parts because there is something cute about a tiny Pekingese carrying a large bear. They'll just have to bite their lips and be firm.

Dogs can get very set in their ways, Wilson adds. A stony silence will help discourage Lady, but her owners will want to change her whole pattern. Wilson recommends rearranging the furniture to take away her hiding place. "They should clear out the treasures and move a chair, bookshelf, or potted plant in the way," she says.

CHAPTER SEVENTEEN

STAYING AT HOTELS

They don't use the weight room, elevators scare them, and they can't figure
out why strangers—some pushing food carts—walk into their rooms.
Dogs can be very polite guests, but only if they know what to expect.

Dogs are indifferent to maid service and the view from the 15th floor, and they certainly don't enjoy spending hours alone in hotel rooms while their owners are off sight-seeing. Taking dogs to hotels is always a challenge—not only for their human companions but also for the bellhops and concierges who have to field complaints about nonstop

barking, or watch in dismay as canine visitors lift their legs on potted plants in the lobby.

"If dogs bark at home, they'll bark twice as much in a hotel; and if they chew on your couch, they'll do damage to a hotel room," says Steve Dale, a radio host at WGN in Chicago, a syndicated columnist, and author of the book *Doggone Chicago.* Even dogs who are perfectly behaved at home get nervous when they visit new places, he explains. Not only are they in strange surroundings but they are also spending quite a lot of time alone. When they get lonely or bored enough, they start looking for ways to vent their emotions, such as scratching at the door, barking, or chewing on table legs.

Dogs are sticklers for routines, Dale adds, and they have a hard time understanding that the rules they follow at home may not apply when they're in a hotel. A dog who always goes outside at 7:00 A.M. to do his business will want to do the same thing in a hotel—even when outside, in his mind, is the carpeted hallway just outside the room.

Staying at hotels doesn't come naturally to dogs, but they learn the ropes quick enough. A bit of planning will ensure that you and your dog can enjoy yourselves without upsetting the other guests.

Comfort Stops

Probably the biggest obstacle to social fitness is the fact that dogs are entirely casual in their bathroom habits. They don't require privacy, and it's easy for them to confuse a vast expanse of carpeting for the yard they use at home. Then there's all that foliage in the lobbies of hotels. It doesn't look any different from the ivy, shrubs, and trees that they visit at home, so they naturally get the wrong idea.

When you check in, you'll want to ask the clerk for directions to dog-friendly locations, Dale says. One hotel near O'Hare Airport in Chicago, for example, offers a garden facility where dogs can sniff and water the flowers—and, if they're interested, watch planes take off and land, as well.

But having a pleasant park nearby doesn't guarantee that dogs won't try to make pit stops somewhere between their rooms and the lobby. To avoid embarrassing breeches of etiquette, here are a few tips from travelers who have learned their lessons the hard way.

Keep moving. Dogs, especially males, rarely just stop and go. Rather, they do some preliminary sniffing—the canine equivalent of opening a magazine. Pausing for even a few seconds when you're taking your dog outside will give him a chance to launch the first part of his bathroom routine, and when that happens, the second part isn't far behind. Once you've put on the leash and are heading through the hotel to the outside, don't stop. Keep walking until you get there, says Gina Spadafori, pet-care columnist for Universal Press Syndicate and author of the book *Dogs for Dummies*.

Many hotels welcome dogs, but you don't want to show up unannounced. When you make reservations, let them know that you'll have company.

Move the leash back and forth. Walking through a hotel lobby isn't the same as walking down the sidewalk, and you'll probably encounter a number of time-eating obstacles, such as knots of people or closed elevator doors. Since every delay in your forward momentum will give your dog an opportunity to do what he shouldn't, you have to find another way to keep him moving. The easiest is to keep moving the leash from hand to hand. This forces him to keep moving even when you're not.

Keep the nose high. You can't teach dogs not to sniff, but you can teach them to keep their noses up—which, for male dogs, is the trick to keeping their rear legs in polite positions. "If they don't sniff, they're not going to lift," Spadafori says.

1. Keep one hand on your dog's collar or leash. As you're walking, be prepared to pull up his head when he starts to sniff.

2. As you lift his head, give a command like "don't touch," and keep walking.

3. When your dog looks up to see what you want, immediately praise him—and keep walking. With some practice, your dog will learn that the command "don't touch" means he should look up and keep moving. And the quicker you move, the fewer problems you'll have.

FAST FIX To prevent accidents in the hallway, elevator, or lobby, give your dog his favorite toy to carry when you leave the room. Dogs who are focused on their toys don't get distracted by their surroundings and are less likely to seek out their next leg-lifting or squatting target, says Spadafori.

Promoting Silence

Dogs take their jobs as family protectors very seriously, and barking comes with the package, says Chris Walkowicz, a judge for the American Kennel Club and author of *The Perfect Match: A Dog Buyer's Guide.* Dogs bark to alert their people to things that are new, scary, or interesting. This is fine at home, but in hotels, dogs find just about everything new, scary, or interesting. This means they bark a lot more than they usually do, and people in adjoining rooms won't be shy about complaining—either to you or to the desk manager. More than a few guests with vocal dogs have found themselves looking for a new hotel because their dogs made too much noise.

Dogs who aspire to social fitness need to understand that barky behavior isn't appropriate in public places. Yelling "Quiet!" usually doesn't help, because dogs interpret this to mean you're challenging them to a barking contest—and they'll bark louder to win. Here's a three-part strategy from Darlene Arden, author of *The Irrepressible Toy Dog*, that's much more effective.

1. When there's a noise outside or someone comes to the door and your dog starts barking, give him some praise after one or two barks. After all, a few barks are hardly unreasonable, and you want him to tell you about potential intruders. Your dog will know from the praise that you heard him and are pleased—and that he doesn't have to keep repeating himself.

2. As soon as you praise your dog, give the command "sit—no bark." The command forces your dog to focus on you instead of whatever it is outside that has his attention.

3. When he sits and stops barking, give him something to eat. The treat will keep his mouth occupied so he can't bark, and it will also reward him for his obedience as well as his silence.

Doing this exercise once or twice a day for a few weeks is usually enough to teach dogs to quit barking on command, Arden says. Dogs can't learn it overnight, however, so you'll want to practice before leaving home.

PLANNING YOUR TRIP

Some hotels cater to dogs and provide great walking trails, gourmet meals, and even grooming services. Many more, however, have closed their doors because too many canine visitors quite literally left their marks. To make sure there aren't any surprises, it's worth making a few calls before you leave home.

Make reservations and get confirmations in writing. "Some places don't have hard and fast rules, and things may change depending on who is at the front desk," says Steve Dale, a radio host at WGN in Chicago, a syndicated columnist, and author of the book *Doggone Chicago*. In addition, hotels sometimes change policies and may refuse to allow dogs, despite what it says in your travel guide.

Describe your dog honestly. Some hotels have size limits, Dale says. These limits will be expressed in different ways, such as, "only small dogs allowed," "only dogs under 30 pounds," or "no taller than your knee." Be sure your dog qualifies, whatever the going definition is.

Take his résumé. Some hotels may require copies of a dog's health certificate. Dale recommends that you take along other credentials, such as diplomas from obedience schools. Even if your dog doesn't look so great on paper, maybe he knows a flashy trick or two. "This may be enough to squeak your 40-pound dog into hotels that only allow 25-pound dogs and smaller."

Alert the staff. The check-in clerks will usually tell the staff, including housekeeping, that you have a dog. But it doesn't hurt to spread the word on your own, says Anne Marie DeStefano, director of sales for the Hotel Pennsylvania in New York City. "We can have extra towels and cleaning supplies available, and we will try to work around your schedule," she says.

Give a little extra. When you're passing out tips, don't forget to leave a few extra bucks when you check out of your room. Tipping is always optional, but it's a nice thing to do since dogs cause extra work for the hotel staff. Your dog may be bathed and coiffed, but he's still a dog, and all dogs shed. This immediately becomes apparent if the room has a white carpet and you have a black dog. Hotels use heavy-duty vacuums, but it still takes elbow grease to remove dog hairs. People don't mind doing extra work when they're getting something extra. You should definitely tip extra if someone has to clean up an accident or otherwise goes out of their way to make your stay comfortable. Any special courtesy performed for your dog surely deserves a bit of recognition.

Stick to the rules. More than a few travelers, desperate for lodging, have sneaked their dogs into no-dog hotels. It's understandable that people do it, but it's risky. You'll be charged extra if you're caught, especially if your dog causes damage.

Dogs who have spent all day in hotel rooms may find it hard to wait until they get outside to do their business. Giving them toys to carry distracts them until they reach the proper place.

Fighting Boredom

New sights and smells will keep dogs entertained for quite a while. Once their initial curiosity winds down, however, they start getting bored, especially when they're left alone for more than a few hours. And bored dogs, like bored children, start looking for things to do, and they're usually not good things.

Probably the most appealing way to pass the time, from a dog's point of view, is by chewing. In hotels, some of the most toothsome targets are remote controls, cushions, and table legs. It's difficult to stop dogs from chewing, because it's natural for them to do it when they're bored or anxious. Rather than trying to stop the behavior, about all you can do is give your dog something more appropriate to focus on, Dale says.

"Bring a favorite toy from home that already has your dog's smell on it," Dale advises. If your dog doesn't have a favorite toy, experiment a bit to see what passes the chew test. Some dogs will chew anything. Others prefer flavored synthetic chews, such as those made by NylaBone. Rawhide isn't a good choice when you're traveling, because many dogs swallow the pieces, which may give them diarrhea.

"You may want to try leaving on the radio or television, depending on your pet's preference," Arden adds. Dogs don't really listen to music or televised conversations, but the familiar sounds will remind them of home and help reduce

boredom and anxiety. In addition, the sounds will help mask outside noises, like doors slamming, that tend to raise canine blood pressures.

For dogs who are left alone, nothing beats the arrival of the housekeepers for a little afternoon excitement. For the housekeepers, however, encountering overly eager dogs is a little too much excitement. And more than a few dogs have taken advantage of their arrival to make a run for it. Arden recommends putting out the "Do not disturb" sign when you leave your dog alone. "You don't want him downstairs running up a bar tab while you're out seeing the sights," she says.

Sleeping in Comfort

Dogs are creatures of habit. They like to eat at the same times and go out at the same times. And at night, they like to sleep in the same places. "If your dog has a blanket or bed, take it with you," says Dale. Even if your dog doesn't have formal sleeping arrangements at home, you'll want to give him something that feels familiar, even if that means tossing one of your used shirts on the floor. Familiar smells relax dogs like nothing else does, and he'll probably curl up on the shirt and go to sleep right away.

"Hotels don't prefer it, but I have no problem with dogs sleeping on the beds as long as they're clean and well-mannered," Arden says. "Besides, if the housekeepers aren't changing the sheets in between guests, you shouldn't be staying there anyway."

Hotels that discourage doggy guests usually make the point that many dogs have fleas, and once fleas are in the room, they're very hard to get rid of. There's some truth to this, so make sure your dog is absolutely flea-free before checking in. These days there are some very safe, effective, and economical anti-flea medications that your veterinarian can recommend, so fleas don't have to be a problem.

A problem that's harder to control is shedding. Every dog sheds a little, and some dogs shed a lot. It's very difficult to remove dog hairs from carpets, furniture, and drapes. If you want your dog—and the thousands of other dogs who will follow—to be welcomed back, you'll want to take a few minutes every day to keep the fur from flying.

• "If your dog sheds big-time, brush him before you go inside the hotel," suggests Dale. "If you have a balcony, brush him every day out there."

Brushing your dog outside or on the hotel balcony will reduce the amount of hair he will shed on the carpets and furniture.

• Take along a blanket or sheet that you can spread over the areas where your dog will be sleeping.

• Before you leave the hotel, clean the room with a hair remover. Pet supply stores sell many different types. The Gonzo Pet Hair Lifter, for example, is a sponge that pulls hair off furniture. The Pet Hair Gatherer keeps carpets clean, and the Helmac Lint Brush easily removes hair from furniture, carpets, and drapes.

FAST FIX The easiest way to remove dog hair from carpets and upholstery is with a strip of masking tape. A small roll will remove tremendous amounts of hair very quickly.

A Space of Their Own

Some of the best-behaved and most well-traveled dogs in America are those who are on the show circuit. Yet even these paragons of good manners, who wouldn't dream of barking at the housekeepers or stealing chocolates off the pillows, usually stay in crates that their handlers take along. It's not so much that they'll misbehave if given too much freedom, but that the crates provide them with comfortable and familiar places where they feel at home, says Arden. "Wouldn't you like to travel with your own private room and bed?" she adds.

People who travel a lot with small dogs usually prefer soft-sided crates because they're easy to carry around. Wire cages and fabric duffle

His own basket. His own toys. Even his own blanket under the bed. All of these touches of familiarity are making this terrier feel right at home.

carriers are also good because they take up very little space. Regardless of the crate you travel with, you have to give your dog time to get used to it before you travel, Arden says. Otherwise, that sparkling new "den" will feel just as scary as the strange hotel room. See chapter twenty for tips on getting your dog used to a crate.

Many hotels, incidentally, prefer that dogs be kept in crates, and some insist on it, says Anne Marie DeStefano, director of sales for the Hotel Pennsylvania in New York City, which hosts thousands of dogs when they arrive for the annual Westminster Kennel Club dog show. Dogs in kennels don't damage rooms, she explains, and the closed door reassures housekeeping folks, who may be afraid of dogs. "Of course, not everyone wants to cage dogs, and it's a hard rule to enforce."

There's one additional thing that everyone who travels with dogs should do, she adds. "The best time to walk dogs at hotels is very early in the morning, before 7:00 A.M." Taking your dog in and out early in the morning means that other guests won't be disturbed. "We also request that you use the service elevator so other guests aren't uncomfortable riding next to a strange dog. People are especially nervous about big dogs," she adds.

Hotels are getting bigger all the time, and some include large expanses of gardens. It's natural for people on vacation to leave the pooper-scooper at home, and when it's 6:00 A.M. and you're the only one out, it's easy to "forget" to clean up what your dog left behind. Eventually, the hotel will be stuck with enough complaints—or shoe-cleaning bills—that dogs will no longer be welcome. So don't forget to put a few bags in your pocket before setting out.

FINDING DOG-FRIENDLY ACCOMMODATIONS

More than a few hotels and vacation spots have literally gone to the dogs and will do everything they can to make you and your canine companion welcome. Upscale hotels such as the Four Seasons, the Ritz Carlton, and Boston's Harbor Hotel offer such amenities as comfortable dog beds and dog-walking services. Some even provide monogrammed doggy-size bathrobes so that you and your dog can lounge in grand—and matching—style.

If you look, you'll find dog-friendly lodgings to fit every pocketbook. Here are a few guides that you can use to help you plan your next trip.

• The Dog Lovers Companion series of books provides the scoop on great—and not-so-great—hotels, parks, beaches, and other places where you can stay with dogs.

"The series is real insider-y about where you can take your dogs legally, where you can go with a wink and nudge, and where you better not try it," says Gina Spadafori, pet-care columnist for Universal Press Syndicate and author of the book *Dogs for Dummies*.

• The *Mobil 1999 Travel Guide on the Road with Your Pet* lists thousands of pet-friendly locations. You can also get information from the American Automobile Association.

• A bimonthly newsletter called "DogGone" publishes dog-friendly travel information based on its database of more than 23,000 pet-friendly destinations, from bed-and-breakfasts, inns, and campgrounds to hotels, ranches, and resorts. Contact editor Wendy Ballard at DogGone, P.O. Box 651155, Vero Beach, FL 32965-1155.

STRANGE behavior

Name SALLY

Breed BEAGLE

Age 5

The Behavior

Sally has always been a barker. Her house is a long way from the nearest neighbor, however, and the noise never bothered her family much. What does bother them are Sally's responses to the grandfather clock they recently inherited. Starting at about noon and continuing until 8:00 or 10:00 at night, Sally howls at the clock when it chimes. And she does it every hour, day after day. Her owners have thought about having a clock maker disconnect the chimes, but they feel that would defeat the whole point of having the clock. They really want to keep the heirloom clock, but the racket is driving them crazy.

The Solution

There's no telling why Sally howls at the clock. Some dogs howl at other dogs. Some howl at sirens. And some apparently howl at clocks.

It's possible that the clock's chimes resemble a howl, and Sally feels the need to howl back, says Liz Palika, a trainer in Oceanside, California, and author of *All Dogs Need Some Training*. It's also possible that the chimes bother Sally's ears, and she howls as a kind of protest. But she doesn't appear to be uncomfortable when she does it, so she's probably just howling because, well, that's what some dogs do.

" 'Quiet' is a must-know command for loud dogs," says Palika. "And beagles are known for being loud. When Sally starts howling, her owners should tell her, 'Sally, quiet.' If she doesn't quiet down immediately, they should say, 'no,' in a low, growly tone of voice. And as soon as she stops howling, they should reward her with a treat." Sally will be faced with a choice. She'll either have to give in to her howling impulses or button up long enough to get the treat. Most dogs will choose the treat.

There is one little complication, however. Sally howls every time the clock chimes. This means her owners will have to be present, commands and treats at the ready, every hour on the hour, at least for a while. It's the only way Sally will make the connection between the command to be quiet and the sound of the clock. It may take a few weeks, but she'll eventually learn to lay off the Big Ben routine, Palika says.

CHAPTER EIGHTEEN

STAYING WITH FRIENDS

Even hosts who love dogs don't always love their behavior—especially when it's the type of behavior they'd never allow in their own dogs. Helping your dog be a proper guest will reduce the risk of social friction and ensure that everyone enjoys the visit.

Most dogs don't travel much. When they do, they probably feel like tourists who have stumbled into a fancy French restaurant with foreign menus and too many forks. Staying with friends is delicate even for people because the rules and expectations are always different than they are at home. The confusion is more pronounced for dogs, which means they're sure to commit all kinds of four-pawed faux pas, like climbing on the couch, complaining when they don't get their usual 5:00 A.M. walks, or, perish the thought, urinating on the corner of an expensive carpet.

This Shetland sheepdog doesn't love the water, but her hosts will appreciate her nice smell and will be more likely to invite her back.

Then there are the human issues you have to deal with. People who love you may not love your dog. And they certainly won't love the social limitations that dogs invariably impose. Their plans may call for a day of sight-seeing followed by a long night out on the town. Your dog, in the meantime, is expecting to be let out at certain times and to have plenty of company the rest of the time. These conflicting agendas can be compromised, but they can't be ignored, says Cheryl S. Smith, a trainer in Port Angeles, Washington, and author of *The Trick Is in the Training*.

There's also the question of whether your dog is truly welcome in your hosts' home, adds Darlene Arden, author of *The Irrepressible Toy Dog*. "If they are dog people, they'll likely be thrilled, but otherwise you could put quite a strain on the friendship," she says.

Arden, who has traveled extensively, has identified a few key areas where host-dog conflicts invariably arise. By anticipating these problems and planning ahead, you can keep your dog happy and keep your friends.

Neat Dogs Get Invited Back

People understand that rules change in different situations, but dogs don't know this. That's why trainers always emphasize consistency—dogs simply can't recognize gray areas. In their minds, nearly everything fits into one of two categories: allowed or forbidden. They can't make distinctions. At home, they drool on the kitchen floor and sprawl on the pillows. So why not in someone else's house?

Since dogs aren't going to change their habits for a 2-day trip, it's up to the people to make the necessary adjustments. Every dog has different habits, but the one thing that has the potential to cause the most conflicts is neatness. Taking care of your dog's personal hygiene is the easiest way to keep everyone happy.

Brush the heck out of her. Even people who love dogs don't love dog hair. The idea of having to vacuum all day after you've gone isn't going to make any host happy. It's worth spending an hour brushing your dog before leaving home, Arden says. While you're at it, give her a bath, too.

Control the slobber. Nature made dogs a little moist around the mouth. They drool when they eat, when they sleep, and when they're getting their bellies rubbed. A little bit of slobber probably won't rub anyone the wrong way, but sloppy splashes on the hardwood floors aren't going to warm your hosts' hearts. You may want to pick up a bib at a pet supply store. Or tie a bandanna around your dog's neck. It shows that your dog is aware of her limitations and is trying to be accommodating. People will appreciate the effort.

Dogs who shed a lot, such as German shepherds, should be brushed thoroughly before they go visiting. You won't get rid of all the loose hair, but grooming will prevent visible messes.

FAST FIX "If you allow your dog on the bed when you're at home, take your own sheet or bedspread for her to lie on," says Smith. Better yet, if she usually uses her own pet bed, take it along. You can put it on the floor next to your bed. She'll feel secure, and you won't have to worry about paying the dry-cleaning bills.

Making the Introductions

Travel is easy when you visit a pet-free family. Things get more complicated when you introduce your dog into someone else's menagerie. Cats aren't a problem because they usually just disappear until you and your pet leave. But dogs will have to deal with the new arrival.

"Dogs are social animals, and for the most part, they really enjoy meeting other dogs," says Norm Costello, D.V.M., a veterinarian in Rancho Sante Fe, California, and owner of Animal Keepers, a chain of upscale kennels in San Diego. But sometimes they don't. That's when people change their plans and start looking for a nearby hotel.

Rather than throwing dogs together and hoping that everyone gets along, Arden recommends starting off with a three-part ritual.

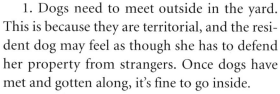

1. Dogs need to meet outside in the yard. This is because they are territorial, and the resident dog may feel as though she has to defend her property from strangers. Once dogs have met and gotten along, it's fine to go inside.

2. Put the dogs on leashes before introducing them. Fights don't occur very often, but even a quick outburst can do a lot of damage—to your nerves as well as to the dogs. Be prepared for a little bit of blustering, which usually gives way to friendship or at least acceptance. If it turns out that the dogs simply can't stand the sight of each other, you'll have to make other plans. They aren't going to get over it in a few days.

3. Stand back while they do their customary sniffing. It's the equivalent of a handshake, and you'll know in a minute or two if the introduction went smoothly. Once the preliminaries are over and the dogs relax, they're probably ready to be friends.

LIVING THE GOOD LIFE

There comes a time in every dog's life when traveling with the family isn't an option. Dog-sitting services are one possibility. Another is to check your dog into a kennel. Kennels have a bad reputation because, for a long time, they tended to be nothing more than outdoor runs with concrete floors. But an increasing number of kennel owners have realized that people aren't satisfied with such rudimentary accommodations. They want their dogs to be comfortable—indeed, pampered.

Enter Animal Keepers, a chain of upscale kennels in San Diego. Each dog has his own suite, and there's a wide range of exercise and play activities, including scheduled romps with other dogs. Water-loving dogs have their choice of kiddie pools in the courtyard. And there are many extras, including toys stuffed with treats and the "yappy hour," in which dogs get their own Frosty Paws ice cream treats.

"It's a change of pace for dogs, and they break down the doors to get in," says Norm Costello, D.V.M., a veterinarian in Rancho Santa Fe, California, and owner of Animal Keepers. "Sometimes, the owners are embarrassed because when it's time to go home, they have a hard time getting them out the door."

All of this opulence isn't free, of course. Traditional kennels typically charge $5 to $10 dollars a day, while the rates at Animal Keepers range from $18 to $21. Clearly, a lot of people don't mind paying a little extra. The upscale kennels have been so successful that Dr. Costello is building an even fancier facility in Orange County, with 15,000 square feet and individual suites that are the size of small living rooms and include raised beds and color televisions. Some rooms will also have video cameras with online hookups that will allow people to periodically check in via the Internet.

A Place to Call Home

Even dogs who are excited by the adventure of staying with new people will often conk out and stay asleep—and out of trouble—for a good part of the trip. That's the best scenario. The worst is when your dog paces, whines, chews the table legs, or has an accident in the corner.

Dogs don't calm down easily, so you'll want to get them settled in first. Take a minute or two to find a place where your dog can hang out when you're gone for the day, if nothing else. Having a place of her own will reduce the risk of household damage, and dogs generally feel happier and more secure when they're tucked into smallish spaces.

People who travel a lot with their dogs often pack baby gates in their cars. These fit in almost any doorway and can be used to cordon off parts of the house. Unlike solid doors, they allow your dog to see where you are and watch what's going on, which helps keep her anxiety to manageable levels.

Your friends may encourage you to confine the dogs—yours and theirs—in the same place. Don't do it, advises Dr. Costello. It's not uncommon for dogs to get along fine when people are around, then terrorize each other when the people are gone. Even if the dogs remain friendly, size differences can be a real issue. You don't want to be in the position of having to explain what happened when your great horse of a dog accidentally sat on her thimble-size companion.

Mary Monteith, a retired school teacher in Bristol, Indiana, discovered for herself the danger of using her host's accommodations for

A baby gate allows dogs to see where everyone is, while keeping them out from underfoot.

her own dog, a Shetland sheepdog named Skye. "During one visit, we fastened Skye to the dog tether in the yard," she says. No one thought about it, but Skye was a lot shorter than the resident dog—so much so that the tether pulled his collar right off his head. "We found Skye up on the highway, headed for home."

Mealtime Etiquette

Dogs don't worry about forks, napkins, or chewing with their mouths open. And because they eat just about anything, no one has to worry about serving them the right foods.

111

Meals away from home would seem like a no-brainer: Put some food in their bowls, and watch them go.

When dogs are by themselves, eating is easy. It gets more complicated when there are other pets around. Problems that you're likely to see may include:

Competition. Dogs consider eating to be a social activity, but they define "social" as merely being in the same place. Otherwise, it's every dog for herself, and they don't hesitate to defend their food.

Theft. In human culture, it's polite to take small servings and make sure that everyone gets their share. Among dogs, however, the rule is to gobble as quickly as possible—and then steal someone else's.

Cat incursions. Given a choice between stealing another dog's food or going for the cat's, dogs always choose the feline fare. For one thing, they won't get beaten up should they get caught in the act. And besides, they think cat food is very tasty.

Ugly messes. The combination of anxiety, excitement, and eating new foods often makes dogs sick. Diarrhea on the carpet isn't any fun at home, and it's mortifying when it happens at someone else's house. Experienced travelers always take a supply of their dog's regular food, says Steve Dale, a radio host at WGN in Chicago, a syndicated columnist, and author of the book *Doggone Chicago.* It's also wise to feed your dog away from where the resident pets are eating, no matter how much your host encourages you to do otherwise. Sure, they'll probably get along, but maybe they won't. Why take the chance?

Nature's Call

You would think that fire hydrants are the same everywhere, but dogs know better. And the idea of making pit stops in unaccustomed places—using this hydrant instead of that one—can be a little too much.

"I live in the country, and my dogs grew up on grass," Smith says. "When I visited people in the city, the dogs would refuse to go to the bathroom. I had to teach them to go on concrete." It works the other way, too—dogs who live in cities may be extremely reluctant to use dirt or grass. They can only hold it for so long, of course. Lost opportunities for pit stops on a morning walk can mean accidents in the house in the afternoon.

Unless your dog has truly remarkable holding power, you're going to have to be patient—and a little creative—to make sure there are no mistakes. Here are a few tips you may want to try.

Multiply by two. If you normally take your dog out twice a day, go four times when you're staying with friends. This will give your a dog a chance to get used to the neighborhood and get over her initial reluctance. The extra exercise will help get things moving, too.

Identify the best places. Just as people travel with itineraries of things to do, your dog needs an itinerary, too. Rather than showing her something different, however, find something similar to what she knows. If you live in the suburbs or the country, for example, find out where the parks are, Smith says. It's not that dogs insist on perfection, but anything that reminds them of home is going to be appreciated.

GETTING ALONG WITH KIDS

Dogs and children go together like peanut butter and jelly—or like oil and vinegar, depending on the mix. Your dog may just want to say, "Hello, hello, I love you," but for children who aren't used to dogs, all of this friendly noise can scare the living hooey out of them, says Steve Dale, a radio host at WGN in Chicago, a syndicated columnist, and author of the book *Doggone Chicago*. Here are a few ways to reduce the potential for social friction.

Tell children to move slowly and speak deeply. An unfortunate consequence of dogs' wild pasts is that they view fast-moving, squeaky things as being eminently chaseable. Young children, with their high voices and high energy levels, can find themselves getting more attention than they want. Unless your dog is used to children or is very well trained, children need to understand that they should move slowly and lower their voices to prevent her from getting too excited.

Stand tall. From a dog's point of view, children, with their small sizes and yippy voices, can easily be confused with puppies, who aren't to be respected. Until everyone gets to know each other, children should be encouraged to stand up when they're around dogs. This makes them appear taller and gives them more status, from the canine point of view. It's hard for children to resist the temptation to get down on all fours to play, but it makes them appear smaller and weaker, and some dogs will instinctively take advantage of the opportunity to push them around.

Pet them under the chin. Unless they know you, dogs don't like being patted on top of their heads. They see this as an act of dominance, and often they won't welcome it, especially from children.

Establish a chain of command. Obedience drills aren't a lot of fun, but they're the best way to teach dogs that they have to listen to all people, including the small ones. It's worth spending 5 to 10 minutes helping the children in the family to give some simple "sit" or "stay" commands. Your dog will figure out that she has to take the kids seriously, and this will reduce the friction later on.

CHAPTER NINETEEN

HIKING

When dogs take to the trail, the most sedate sidewalk strollers can turn into leash-straining bundles of trouble. A little pre-hike training and a few tricks will ensure that jaunts in the woods are a pleasure for everyone.

Even dogs who have spent their entire lives in cities, sniffing the same few blocks of sidewalk, undergo a transformation when they take to the trail. They revel in the fresh air and open land and nearly go out of their minds as they discover for themselves the thousands of intriguing smells that their ancestors smelled every day.

It's difficult for even the best-trained dogs to control themselves, and many don't even try. As soon as they're out of the car, it's as though they forget every command they ever knew. They bark wildly at squirrels, butterflies, and falling leaves. They surge up the trail, scattering hikers left and right. They run so much and get so excited that they're overwhelmed before they top the first hill. That's about when they plop down and seem to say, "You go ahead. I'll just wait for the first cab right here."

There's a lot more freedom on the trail than on a crowded city street, which is why people take their dogs hiking in the first place. But even in the wilderness, there are a few basic rules of doggy comportment, says Cheryl S. Smith, a trainer in Port Angeles, Washington, and author of *On the Trail with Your Canine Companion*. Rangers get complaints every year about barking, menacing, or merely overexuberant dogs. And hundreds of owners find themselves apologizing for their dogs' unruly behavior—and vowing never to take them hiking again.

BREED SPECIFIC

Dalmatians are among the best hiking dogs because they've been bred to travel far and fast—which is why they were the dogs of choice for early fire companies. Pekingese and other short-nosed breeds often have a hard time on the trail because their breathing isn't very efficient and they get winded easily.

Under Control

Nearly all of the behavior problems that occur on the trail could be prevented by the simple expedient of putting dogs on leashes, Smith says. Unless you do your hiking out of season or in extremely remote places, your dog is going to meet other hikers. Even people who own dogs themselves can't be sure if this 40-pound bundle of excitement rocketing toward them is friendly or not. And *their* dogs may not be sure, either.

Keeping dogs on leashes is the rule on most public lands—not only for the comfort of other hikers, but for the health of the dogs themselves. "Dogs have been shot for chasing wildlife; and since a lot of public hiking areas are also grazing areas, you have to be careful all the time," Smith says.

Dogs on leashes still get to enjoy the outdoors, she adds. They have innumerable opportunities to sniff and be sniffed, and they receive a lot of compliments for their impressive manners. This is assuming, of course, that your dog is used to a leash in the first place. If she's not, a pleasant hike has a way of deteriorating into a shoulder-wrenching afternoon as you try to go one way while your dog is determined to go the other.

Dogs don't need formal obedience training to get trail-ready, Smith says. Here's a crash course that you can start—and complete—a day or two before setting out.

• Before leaving home, take your dog for two or three walks a day. Put on the leash like you always do and head down the street.

• When your dog surges ahead, brace your feet and pull your arms in close to your body for support. "You don't have to say anything," Smith says. "Just stand there like a post." Dogs don't like the sensation of straining without making progress and will quickly back off a bit.

• When your dog relaxes and there's slack in the leash, say, "Good close," Smith says. Then continue your walk.

Dogs who are set in their ways will strain forward and hit the ends of their leashes repeatedly. "You'll have to stop again and repeat the process until she gets the idea," Smith explains. A few

Dogs should be expected to lighten the load for their human companions by carrying their own food and water in doggy backpacks.

115

Dogs usually walk on the left of their owners. But when you're hiking, it's useful to teach them to swap sides on command so that they can get out of the way of oncoming hikers.

whom, it seemed, had been coached in the finer points of etiquette. "I'd been looking forward to spending a few days just listening to the silence," she says. "But the barking never stopped, and twice I got hit in the knees by dogs zooming up from behind."

There aren't a lot of rules that dogs need to know to be good outdoor citizens, Smith explains. The basics include:

Keep the noise down. You can't expect dogs in the wilderness to act like librarians, but no one wants to listen to cacophonies of canine choruses. Dogs need to understand that while some barking is acceptable, too much is a problem. "Dogs will stop barking when you place your hand on top of their muzzles," Smith says. "After a while, they learn that this is the signal to be quiet."

Walk side by side. Wilderness trails are often too narrow for people and dogs to pass in comfort. Even dogs who stick by their owners will block passersby who approach on the left—the side on which dogs are trained to walk. To avoid collisions, Smith says, it's helpful to teach dogs to move to either side. Use the leash to direct your dog to the side that you want her on, then tell her, "Side," while motioning to your thigh. Most dogs will quickly learn to associate the word with the gesture and will happily move to the required side, Smith says.

Make the introductions. Trail life is filled with uncertainties, and for many hikers, a big unknown is whether approaching dogs are friendly or not. You have to help your dog understand that she needs to wait for your signal

days of practice aren't going to make your dog a candidate for the Westminster dog show, but they're enough to get her comfortable with the leash and will allow both of you to enjoy the outdoors a little more.

Manners on the Trail

Nearly every hiker can tell stories about weekends that literally went to the dogs. Molly Hopkins, a landscape architect in Albuquerque, New Mexico, remembers a hike in New Mexico's Pecos National Historical Park when nearly everyone she encountered had dogs—none of before approaching other people or dogs. "When I see people with dogs coming my way, I usually ask them if their dogs would like to meet mine," Smith says. "Sometimes, the dogs really enjoy it, and you never know, you may make a friend."

Let strangers pass. Since the narrowness of wilderness trails makes it difficult for people to keep their distance, the social thing for dogs to do is step aside when people approach, Smith says. This is especially helpful when you're on a trail with bicyclists or runners, because they can trigger a dog's chase instinct. "I always have the dogs sit when bicyclists approach or when other people have dogs that they aren't controlling very well," Smith says.

Canine Outfitters

Just as you expect people you hike with to carry their own belongings, your dog should pull her weight, too. As more and more dogs take to the woods, pet supply and hiking stores have begun stocking quite an array of canine hiking gear. You'll want to add a few extra items to your pack as well. Here's a rundown of what every trail dog needs.

A nylon collar and cloth leash. Metal choke collars tend to snag on brush; and because leather leashes absorb sweat, they act like magnets for porcupines and other critters, Smith says. She recommends using a flat nylon quick-release collar and a nylon or cloth leash.

Bug protection. When one dog is scratching because of fleas, it won't be long before every dog that she encounters is scratching, too. Smith recommends spritzing dogs with a flea spray before you hit the trail. Veterinarians often recommend sprays containing pyrethrins, which are safer than some chemical sprays. "I spray some onto a rag and then wipe the dog with it so I can control where the spray goes," Smith says.

Boots. A dog with sore feet isn't going to walk very far, which means that the people in the party will either have to stop before they're ready or carry her to the camp. To ensure that your dog keeps up, you may want to fit her with protective boots, available in pet supply stores. Most dogs don't like wearing boots, so you may want to borrow a set from someone to see if your dog will put up with them.

Many wilderness trails are narrow, so it's courteous to step aside with your dog and let others pass.

Food pack. Since your dog won't cook dinner or set up the tent, the least she can do is carry her own food, along with collapsible food and water dishes. Many pet supply and camping stores sell sidesaddle packs that are contoured to fit around a dog's rib cage. "Even a little dog is capable of carrying her own food," Smith says.

Packs take some getting used to because they make dogs a little wider than usual, Smith adds. This can confuse dogs when they're walking off-trail. "Some dogs are always surprised when they don't fit through the usual spaces."

Dotting the I's

Most hikes don't require a lot of preparation beyond packing food, fresh water, and perhaps some Dramamine for the drive to the trail. But your dog will have a much better time if you take care of a few additional details.

• If your dog's only exercise lately has been walking around the block, you'll want to spend some time getting her into shape for the trek, says Smith. She recommends taking longer walks than usual in the weeks before leaving, preferably walks that involve going up and down hills. Long walks are good because you'll be taking them on your trip.

• Ask your veterinarian to make sure that your dog is up for the trip. While you're

Pet supply stores sell I.D. capsules that attach to your dog's collar and contain information on where you're staying and how to contact you should your dog become lost.

Why do dogs eat dung?

Even dogs who are picky about food will eagerly sample the droppings that other animals leave behind. Veterinarians aren't sure why they do it, but they suspect that it's one of three things.

1. Early training. Mother dogs often keep their nests clean by eating the stools of the pups, and dogs learn by watching.

2. Nutrition. Some dogs may not get all of the nutrients that they need from their food, and dung is filled with usable proteins, vitamins, and minerals.

3. Taste. Dogs have 215 million more scent receptors than people, and it's possible that the scent and flavor of dung provides a taste sensation that people can't—or don't want to—imagine.

at the vet's office, get a copy of your dog's health certificate and proof of vaccinations. Some campgrounds and border crossings won't let dogs pass unless they have the proper documentation, Smith says.

• Your dog's usual identification tags won't do you a whole lot of good if she gets lost, because you won't be home to get the call. Smith recommends equipping your dog with temporary identification—something that tells people where you're staying or what the campground number is. Pet supply stores sell small containers that hook on to pets' collars and contain papers that list your current location, your destination, and your contact information.

STRANGE behavior

Name RICKI

Breed BORDER COLLIE

Age 3

The Behavior

Ricki and her family go camping several times a year. While the adults are hiking or cooking supper, the children collect sticks, which they use for swordplay, building forts, and roasting marshmallows. Ricki, unfortunately, likes sticks even more than the kids do. So she steals them. When the children try to take them back, Ricki resorts to tug-of-war. Her attitude seems to be that the winner takes all—or at least half. The children get mad, Ricki gets yelled at, and the adults are sick of the whole thing. Except for her stick-athons, Ricki is a gentle dog and careful around the kids. No one understands why she has this grabby side or what they can do to stop it.

The Solution

Dogs act in mysterious ways. No one will ever know why Ricki focuses all of her attention on sticks. But her single-minded pursuit isn't unusual, especially among Border collies, who tend to be a little obsessive, says Betty Fisher, a trainer based in San Diego and co-author of *So Your Dog's Not Lassie*. "They have intense personalities and a very single-minded nature."

It's likely that Ricki will never give up her passion for sticks, Fisher explains. The challenge for the family is to make her more discriminating in her choice of sticks. She recommends that the adults (not the children, who won't have enough authority or control) practice a simple obedience drill: They should have Ricki sit and stay, then throw a stick for her to chase—and praise her when she chews or runs around with it. With practice, Ricki will learn that only sticks that are thrown are hers. Sticks that are on the ground or being used as marshmallow skewers are someone else's.

At first, Ricki will try to extend her privilege to all sticks, Fisher says. She may even get pretty pushy about it. She should be ignored. Praise should only be given when she plays with her stick. She'll have a hard time telling the difference at first. So she should probably stay on a leash so she doesn't get a chance to rediscover the joy of stick grabbing. If Ricki is successful at grabbing even one stick that she shouldn't, she may decide that that's the best way to get them after all.

CHAPTER TWENTY

AIRLINE ETIQUETTE

Flying is stressful even for seasoned travelers. It's worse for dogs.
They can't wander the aisles or watch in-flight videos. They need a little extra
help to stay comfortable and calm.

Most dogs are required by airlines to travel in the cargo hold, but small dogs may qualify as carry-on luggage. This means that they get to fly in comfort in the cabin, and they make great portable companions—unless they happen to get frustrated when their canine urges to explore and sniff are thwarted or when they're simply scared to death. That's when they start panting, barking, or whining. That's no fun for you, for them, or for the other people on the plane.

Dogs aren't like laptop computers, which can be pushed under a seat when you want a break. But they can be taught to relax and enjoy the flight. In fact, show dogs log more frequent-flier miles than most people and quickly get used to the routine, says Alan Resnick, editor in chief of *Dogs in Canada* magazine.

Working with Instincts

Dogs who ride in the cabin must be small enough to fit in a container that will fit under the seat. In most cases, the upper limit is about 19 inches high. You can buy airline-approved carriers at pet supply stores. Carriers made from hard plastic, such as the Vari-Kennel (size 100), will fit under most airline seats. So will soft-sided bags such as the Sherpa Bag.

People cringe at the idea of spending hours in such tight quarters, but dogs feel differently because they have an instinct called denning. They're most comfortable in small, cozy spaces. Once dogs understand that their carriers are dens, they view them as wonderful retreats and

He'll never love flying, but planning and preparation have turned this Belgian sheepdog into a seasoned traveler.

look forward to spending time there—not only at 30,000 feet but back home as well, says Resnick.

Dogs don't automatically take to new dens, however. It takes a little work to make a house a home.

• A few weeks before your trip, leave the carrier in the living room or bedroom so that your dog can explore it at his leisure. Putting a few treats or a favorite toy inside will pique his interest and help him associate the carrier with nice things.

• Once your dog is happily climbing in and out of the carrier—or, better yet, is taking little naps inside it—close it for a while. He may get a little nervous at first, but if you encourage him and make it all seem like fun, he'll start to relax. Keep him in the carrier for 10 to 15 minutes, then give him a great treat when you let him out. Do this two or three times a day, gradually increasing the crate time in half-hour increments.

• Keep practicing until he can stay in the crate for about 3 hours without getting upset. This is about the length of many plane trips. "Dogs have no concept of time," says Alan Alford, owner of Fresh Pond Travel in Marlborough, Massachusetts, a

RULES AND REGULATIONS

Whether your dog will ride in the cabin or in the belly of the plane, plan on spending about $50 each way. You also need a current health certificate and rabies vaccination record. And since most dogs fly belowdecks, you need to plan for their comfort and safety.

• Only a few dogs are allowed on each flight, usually on a first-come, first-served basis. So plan on arriving at least 2 hours before departure. Be sure to check your dog in with your regular luggage as "excess baggage." Don't send him "freight" because freight may not travel on the same flight as you.

• The flight crew can monitor the atmosphere in the cargo hold, so it's worth asking them to watch out for your dog while you're in the air.

• Airline crates have containers for water, but this usually gets spilled fairly quickly. "I put a doggy treat in one cup and fill the other cup with water and freeze it," says Chris Walkowicz, a judge for the American Kennel Club and author of *The Perfect Match: A Dog Buyer's Guide.* "The dog has ice to lick, but water won't slosh out and make a mess."

• Lining the crate with layers of newspaper and putting cedar shavings on top will help keep dogs comfortable. "It smells good and also contains any mess if the dog uses the bathroom or gets sick," Walkowicz says.

Dogs who are going to fly need to get used to traveling in crates. When they're introduced to the crates gradually, they'll come to see them as safe, secure dens.

121

company that specializes in booking travel arrangements for show dogs. "They don't recognize the difference between 2 hours and 12 hours."

In-Flight Manners

Some dogs take to air travel as easily as they sneak up on the couch, but others start getting nervous even before they leave home—and the sounds and smells of a busy airport can just about put them over the edge. The only way to keep them calm (and quiet) in the air is to keep them occupied, Resnick says.

Treat them little and often. Dogs who have big meals before flying are likely to deposit most of the food on the floor of the crate. But their stomachs won't object to small amounts of food, and the excitement of getting treats will keep their minds occupied. Resnick recommends taking along a hollow toy that's loaded with sticky cheese or peanut butter. Most dogs forget their fears when they're given something good to play with and eat—and dogs who are eating can't bark or whine, he explains.

Be nonchalant. Dogs are very good at picking up signals from their owners. When you're tense and nervous about how they're feeling, they get even more anxious. It's fine to reassure a nervous dog, but you should keep your voice low and calm and act as though nothing is out of the ordinary, Resnick says.

Make friends with your neighbor. Even though airline regulations don't permit dogs to

The Parachuting Pooch

Brutus loves to fly. In fact, this 10-pound miniature dachshund loves it so much that he does it without a plane. That's okay because his owner, Ron Sirull of Phoenix, Arizona, flies without a plane, too. A parachutist who promotes special events, Sirull has discovered that parachuting with Brutus really makes people notice.

Brutus doesn't have his own parachute (he can't pull a rip cord), but he doesn't need one, because Sirull hooks him up to a harness, puts on his special goggles, and tucks him inside a chest pouch on his jumpsuit. On the way down, Brutus's lips flap into a grin with the rushing wind.

Despite the thrill of hurtling downward at 35 miles an hour, parachuting is a very safe sport—although Sirull thinks it may have had some effect on Brutus's diminutive stature. "He used to be taller," Sirull jokes, "but we had a couple of hard landings."

step out of their carriers, there may be some unofficial leeway, especially if the people who are sitting around you don't mind a little canine company. "Whether you follow the rule is a matter of your conscience and the patience of the person you're sitting next to," says Alford. As long as your dog is quiet and keeps a low profile, many travelers won't object.

FAST FIX The quickest way to calm a puppy who's leaving home and flying for the first time is to surround him with a familiar scent. Resneck recommends lining the crate with a blanket from home. "Rub the blanket over Mom dog and the other puppies so you have a nice reminder of home that your new puppy can curl up in," he suggests.

STRANGE behavior

Name GORDY

Breed DALMATIAN

Age 6

The Behavior

Gordy has a one-way mind. His bed and food dish are on the lower level of a split-level home, and he eagerly runs downstairs when it's time to eat or go to bed. But for some reason, he doesn't realize that the stairs are exactly the same going up as coming down. When it's time to climb up, he freezes and starts trembling. Eventually, he makes the climb, but he never likes to do it. His owners suspect that he's re-membering the time when he fell down the stairs several years before. They've tried yelling, cajoling, and dragging him up the stairs, but no dice. He's still terrified.

The Solution

"Dalmatians are the elephants of the dog world," says Judith Halliburton, a trainer and behaviorist in Albuquerque, New Mexico, and author of *Raising Rover*. "They have incredible mem-ories and rarely forget a traumatic incident like a fall."

Actually, any dog can develop a phobia, and the fear often makes even less sense than Gordy's. Some dogs are terrified of lampposts or curbs. Some are afraid of hats or run away from men with beards or cower when they see people in uniform. Even the rustling of paper will put some dogs into a panic. In some ways, Gordy's owners are lucky. His fear does have some basis in reality, which gives them something specific to overcome.

"The way to solve this dog's problem is, literally, one step at a time," says Halliburton. "They should have him sit at the bottom of the stairs. Just that little command is going to lessen his anxiety because he'll think, 'Good, something I can do.'"

After Gordy sits, they'll need to tempt him upward with something very special. Halli-burton recommends putting a bit of dried liver—Gordy's favorite food—on the first step. He may hesitate, but sooner or later, his taste-buds will urge him upward. When he climbs up to grab the food, he should be made to sit again. At this point, his owners will want to reward and praise the heck out of him, then give it up for the day.

Each day, they should help Gordy climb another step, lured by liver. "It's going to take at least as many days as there are steps," Halliburton says.

☆ SPECIAL SKILLS ☆

FIND THE CAR

It's not a trick that you can use at the mall, but when you're out in the country and far from the nearest road, you can depend on your dog to find his way back to the car. With a little training, he'll even be able to pick out your car among dozens of nearly identical makes and models.

1 Put your dog on a leash and walk him to the car several times a day for a few days. Touch the metal, say "car," and give him a treat. When he starts perking up when he hears "car," have him touch the car with his nose or paw, and give him a reward.

Starting from the yard or the end of the block, tell your dog, "Find the car," and walk him to it. When he touches the car, give him a treat. Keep practicing for several days.

2 Rub the bottom of your shoe with a piece of hot dog and walk toward your car. Encourage your dog when he sniffs around your feet, and keep encouraging him as he follows your trail to the car. Give him a great reward when he makes it to the car and touches it with his nose or paw.

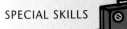

★ SPECIAL SKILLS ★

GET THE PAPER

Dogs love to carry things in their mouths, and sometimes they'll even bring them back. They especially love retrieving newspapers because they're easy to carry. And because the paper arrives every day, your dog will always have something to look forward to.

1 Make a "training paper" by rolling the newspaper tightly and wrapping it with tape. Toss it a few feet away, and say, "Get the paper!" As your dog gets more skilled, start tossing the paper where it usually lands. Make sure that your dog sees you throw it.

2 Once your dog has the hang of chasing and retrieving the paper, start putting it on the ground when he's not around. Then bring him out, show him the paper, and say, "Get the paper!" At this point, he'll be ready to take the final step—looking for and retrieving the newspaper no matter where it lands.

PUSH THE ELEVATOR BUTTON

Many hotels welcome dogs, but other guests may not, especially when you're all crammed into an elevator and riding to the 53rd floor. A fun way to break the ice is to ask your dog to push the "close door" button. Assuming that your dog is tall enough to reach the button, it's an easy lesson to teach.

1 Begin by teaching your dog to put his front feet on the wall. Stick a small cardboard circle on the wall at about the same height as an elevator button. Pat the spot and say, "Feet up!" With a little practice, your dog will learn to hit the spot every time. When he hits it, say, "Button!" Also give him a lot of praise.

2 Once your dog makes the connection between the "button" on the wall and the real buttons in the elevator, he'll be sure to have an appreciative audience as he rides from floor to floor.

☆ S P E C I A L   S K I L L S ☆

SAY THANK YOU

Most dogs know a few social niceties, but only a few understand the importance of saying thank you. By giving a polite bow when people do nice things, your dog will always get a first-class reception.

1 While your dog is standing, kneel or sit on the floor next to him. Put one hand under his tummy to support his rear end. With the other hand, show him a treat and hold it under his nose.

While keeping his rear up with one hand, slowly move the hand with the treat down toward the floor. Where the treat goes, his nose will follow. As he moves his nose down, say, "Thank you." Then give him the treat and a lot of praise.

2 When his front end is all the way down, tell him, "Stay," so he holds the position for a few seconds.

PART FIVE

MEETING THE NEIGHBORS

These days, most dogs live in cities and suburbs. This means they have to get familiar with situations that their ancestors never thought about, like meeting cats without chasing them, and doing their business in parks and not on the sidewalk.

CHAPTER TWENTY-ONE

LIFE ON A LEASH

In an ideal world, dogs would run free. But dogs today have to deal with traffic and busy sidewalks, not to mention local laws. They need to know how to act on leashes. When they do it well, their people are happy, and they get to go out more often.

No dog has ever captured the essence of social fitness as well as Lassie. No matter what adventures the scriptwriters come up with, this wonderful collie behaves impeccably. She never jumps on people, barks when she isn't supposed to, sniffs people in embarrassing places, or tugs when Jeff or Timmy walk her on a leash—not that she is on a leash very often.

If Lassie lived in the real world instead of on television, she'd spend a lot more time attached to one end of a human-to-canine tether. The wide-open lands of yesteryear have been covered over with shopping malls, housing developments, and four-lane highways. Modern environments are simply too crowded and dangerous for dogs to navigate safely on their own.

In any event, most dogs don't have anywhere near the self-control that Lassie has. Leashes

Good leash training has made these Italian greyhounds well-mannered walkers rather than a handful of trouble.

make it possible for people to keep tabs on their dogs when the dogs would prefer to be doing something else. Moreover, many local governments now have laws requiring dogs to be on leashes when they're out in public. Like it or not, leashes are a fact of life for most dogs today.

Ties That Bind

Leashes may be necessary, but they aren't without hassles for dogs or their owners. From a dog's point of view, wearing a leash and collar is an unwelcome restraint and sometimes a literal pain in the neck. For you, a leash is more likely to be a pain in the shoulder as you pull one way and your dog pulls another. Even when there isn't outright resistance, a walk around the block gets complicated when:

• The leash gets tangled around your legs—or, more often, around your dog's legs—like a Chinese jump rope.

• Your dog pulls so hard on the leash that you feel as though you're training for the chariot race in *Ben-Hur*.

• Your dog suddenly decides to sniff and anoint a tree. When you're walking slowly, this isn't a problem. If you happen to be running, the abrupt braking action can cause you to fall on your face.

• Your dog sees something that puzzles or worries her and stops in her tracks to investigate. She won't move, and neither can you.

• In a valiant attempt to obey leash and pooper-scooper laws at the same time, you engage in a public version of Twister as you struggle to manage the leash and a plastic bag at the same time.

Leash walks will never be as easy as wandering freely in the country or throwing balls in a leashes-optional park. But it doesn't have to be a maddening experience, either. Leashes rarely come with instructions because the principles are pretty simple. But the execution takes a little practice.

What Works for You

Trainers sometimes give the impression that using a leash is a precision art and that everyone should be able to walk down the street in lockstep with their dogs. True, the classic heeling position, in which dogs are practically attached to their owners' left legs, looks nice in dog shows. But this is rarely necessary in real life. There's nothing wrong with having your dog amble somewhere alongside you on a loose leash, says Robin Kovary, director of the American Dog Trainers Network in New York City.

Depending on how much you want to work with your dog, you can achieve as much (or as little) precision as you wish. People who live

This Australian shepherd is totally focused on his owner, whether he's on or off the leash.

in cities and walk on crowded sidewalks usually want their dogs right by their sides. Those who do their walking in suburbia are generally more flexible.

There's no real reason for your dog to always walk on your left side, adds Sarah Wilson, a trainer in Gardiner, New York, and co-author of *Childproofing Your Dog*. This practice originated with hunters. Since they carried their guns over their right forearms, they wanted their dogs on the left for safety. Trainers continue this custom mainly because it's more convenient when all of their students are positioned in the same way.

BREED SPECIFIC

Walking on a leash isn't exactly rocket science, but for some dogs, it may as well be. Siberian huskies have a hard time learning not to pull, because they've been bred to be power plants for sleds. Herding dogs such as shelties (left) tend to run ahead—a genetic throwback to their urges to herd lost sheep—and retrievers want to indulge their tracking instincts by keeping their noses close to the ground.

"There's no magic to this," Wilson says. "It really doesn't matter whether your dog is walking on your right or left side."

There is one aspect of leash training in which there's very little leeway: You need to be consistent. "The rules for walking your dog need to be very clear," says Kimberly Barry, Ph.D., a certified applied animal behaviorist in Austin, Texas. "Consistent training in a positive manner is the key."

Buying a Leash

A leash is nothing more than a tether that links you and your dog together. It can be as simple as a length of rope attached to a bandanna or as beautifully intricate as a braided leather lead attached to a jeweled collar. Style and appearance are certainly one way to choose a leash. More important is function. Different leashes and collars do different jobs. Having the right equipment makes walking your dog a lot more fun. The wrong equipment makes things tough. You won't have much fun if the leash is hurting your hands, and your dog won't have much fun if the collar is hurting her neck.

Regardless of the style, you probably want a leash that's 6 feet long. This is long enough to give dogs freedom to sniff, and short enough to keep them under control. Longer leashes—up to 50 feet in some cases—are good when you're teaching puppies to come, but they're too unwieldy for regular walks.

Nylon or cotton leashes. These have many advantages. They're lightweight, fold easily into a pocket, and are inexpensive. But they're not very comfortable for the people holding them. "Nylon tends to be very slippery, and cotton webbing can give a nasty rope burn," says Deborah Manheim, a professional dog walker in Brooklyn, New York.

Leather leashes. Many people have love-hate relationships with leather leashes. They're heavy; they absorb odors; and they're slow to dry once they get wet. They're also three or four times the price of nylon leashes. Still, many trainers only use leather leashes—in part because they last almost forever, and also because they're comfortable to hold, Manheim says.

Retractable leashes. The main reason that people dislike leashes is that they restrict their dogs' ability to run and explore. Retractable leashes have solved this problem. Ranging in length from about 16 to 32 feet, retractable leashes allow you to play out extra line when the

coast is clear, then zip it back in when you want your dog closer. People who own retractable leashes usually love them, but the convenience of freedom comes with a price. The leashes have thick plastic handles that are hard to get a grip on and can be uncomfortable to hold. "I prefer not to use them because if a dog is a puller, the retractable leash encourages this behavior," Manheim adds.

Another problem with retractable leashes has nothing to do with you or your dog, but with other people in the area. The lines are very thin and hard to see. More than a few people have walked between people and their dogs—and tripped because they never saw the leashes.

Specialty leashes. Manufacturers have created an astonishing variety of gear for pets (and people) with special needs. People with arthritis who have trouble holding a leash, for example, may use a product called PuppyPull, which

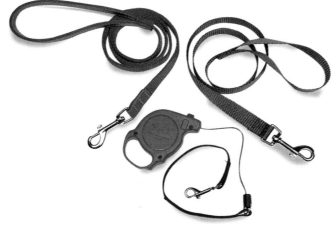

Choosing a leash has more to do with your personal style than with the type of dog you have. Top left and right: nylon leashes; bottom: retractable leash.

wraps around the waist and leaves the hands free. For dogs with arthritis or hip problems, there's a leash called Bottom's Up. It slightly raises the dog's rear end as she walks, which helps support her weight.

Couplers. If you're walking two or three small dogs and you don't feel like wrestling with multiple leashes, you'll probably want a coupler. Couplers have two ends: One end attaches to the leash, and the other end has multiple clips that allow you to hook on to several collars. Couplers are convenient and less expensive than buying several leashes. But the collar ends usually aren't

133

From left: slip or choke collar; nylon collar with plastic clasps; cotton webbing and leather collars in two different sizes.

long enough, so the dogs are always banging into each other. And they don't provide a lot of control, Manheim says.

Buckle collars. Usually made from leather or nylon, these are flat collars that you can adjust in the same way you would a belt. "They are ideal for small, delicate, and sensitive dogs, including puppies, and for adult dogs who walk nicely on a leash," says Kovary.

Head halters. Buckle collars don't give much control when you're working with assertive or unruly dogs. An alternative is the head halter. Made from soft nylon webbing, head halters have two parts: a loop that encircles a dog's muzzle, and a strap that goes behind her neck. They're designed in such a way that when a dog lunges forward, the nose loop pulls her head down and makes her lose her balance. After crashing into herself a few times, even the most headstrong dog learns not to pull against the leash.

"They're similar to horse bridles, which operate on the same principle: Where the head goes, the body must follow," Kovary explains. "They're very good for dogs who bark a lot when they're walking, who lunge at other dogs or people, or who walk along the sidewalk with their heads down in search of goodies."

The webbing on head halters is soft, but it still presses and rubs. Most dogs need a few weeks to get used to it.

Slip collars. Also called choke collars, these have traditionally been recommended by almost all trainers. They're designed in such a way that pulling the leash causes the collar to briefly tighten. This puts uncomfortable pressure on a dog's neck and also makes a jingling sound that dogs dislike. It's an effective way to correct them when they make mistakes.

Attitudes about slip collars have changed in recent years. Trainers still recommend them for dogs who are very independent or headstrong and don't readily respond to commands. "A slip collar may be the only thing that gets her attention," Kovary says. But for most dogs, the collars aren't necessary because there

A body harness is a comfortable alternative to a collar and leash, especially for puppies, small or delicate dogs, or dogs with back problems.

are better ways to help them learn. In addition, slip collars can damage the windpipe when they aren't used properly.

"Slip collars can be very hard on a dog," Kovary says. "A large percentage of dogs don't need them, and a large percentage of owners don't know how to use them."

Body harnesses. Puppies and small dogs have delicate throats and windpipes that can be injured by conventional collars. They often do better with body harnesses. Usually made of nylon webbing, harnesses embrace the torso rather than the neck. Even if you give the leash a stout pull, the pressure will be distributed over a wide area. This makes harnesses more comfortable and safer than conventional collars. And because the harnesses provide back support, they're often recommended for dogs with spinal problems.

Nighttime collars. A lot of people don't get home until dark, which makes the usual walk-the-dog ritual somewhat hazardous. Pet supply stores sell battery-powered collars with flashing lights. The flashes are quite bright and make dogs visible to cars from blocks away.

The mere sight of a leash is enough to launch most dogs into happy orbits. This fox terrier has learned that if she doesn't stand quietly, she doesn't get the walk.

Taming the Leash

Until someone designs a leash that automatically walks dogs around the block and cleans up after them, people will continue to be attached to one end while their dogs have a great time at the other. There are thousands of trainers and obedience schools in the United States, and most communities have basic-skills classes going on nearly every night. Obedience classes are great places to learn the basics of leash

control, but there are a few things that aren't always taught. For example:

Launch quietly. It's impossible for children to be calm when they see Christmas presents under the tree, and it's just as hard for dogs to relax when the leash comes out of the closet. They get so excited, in fact, that it's a challenge just to attach the leash, much less have a tranquil walk. "Proper leash deportment begins before you even put on the leash," Kovary says.

She recommends getting your dog in the right frame of mind by having her sit or lie down. Listening to you and obeying simple commands will focus her attention, Kovary explains. When you aren't in the mood for a struggle, you can simply hang out until she settles down on her own. Either way, don't attach the leash until the manic energy has cooled somewhat.

135

The most efficient way to hold a leash is to put your thumb through the loop and lay the strap across your palm.

Put your thumb through the loop. Rather than holding the end of the leash as they walk, many people slip their wrists through the loop at the end or wrap the whole thing a few times around their wrists. This keeps your hands free and reduces finger fatigue, but it can also get you hurt, especially if you have a large dog. "If you lose your balance and the leash is wrapped around your wrist, you can't let go of the leash easily," Wilson explains.

The best way to hold a leash is to put your thumb through the loop and drape the end of the strap across your palm. Use your other hand to hold and support the middle of the leash. This position gives you enough leverage to control your dog and is still comfortable enough for long walks, Wilson explains.

Practice control. Once your dog is calm, the leash is attached, and the door is open, it's

Proper leash etiquette requires that dogs walk next to or slightly ahead of people.

time to start working on your basic moves. Dogs need time to get used to leash walks, Kovary says. Until they've had a few lessons, they won't have the foggiest idea what they're supposed to do. To help your dog make the connection between the leash and walking properly, here's a three-part plan that Kovary recommends.

1. As you walk, keep looking at your dog and encourage her along. This isn't to be social, but to focus her attention on you. "Everything outside is going to be a big magnet for her attention. You want to do everything you can to make yourself the biggest magnet out there."

2. Using both hands to manipulate the leash, encourage your dog to walk next to or slightly ahead of you. The idea isn't to pull her around a lot, but to help her understand where her personal space is and what her boundaries are.

A Dog Walker's Life

While thousands of her fellow New Yorkers are getting their workouts in health clubs, Deborah Manheim is getting hers in the street, thanks to the dozens of straining, pulling, exuberant dogs she takes for walks each day. A professional dog walker in Brooklyn, Manheim exercises as many as five dogs at a time. That can add up to 350 pounds of pulling canine weight. After a half-hour, she swaps one group of dogs for another, and then another—and she does it for 4 to 8 hours a day.

It can be a challenge to walk even one dog on Brooklyn's crowded streets.

Walking five of them requires dexterity, a strong arm, and an intimate understanding of dogs.

"You need to know who's dominant and who's submissive," she says. "If I have two rambunctious dogs, I have to think about the group and maybe not walk those two together."

Manheim has learned that it doesn't require huge amounts of strength to control her charges. But it does require savvy. "It's totally cool to be controlling a pack of dogs while walking past a 6-foot-3 guy with one unruly Lhasa apso," she says.

"When your dog walks alongside you, she'll be less likely to wrap the leash around you."

3. When you slow down or stop, your dog should match your pace. She won't understand this at first. You can help her make the connection by putting your palm in front of her face as you stop. She'll automatically slow down, and that's when you'll want to give instructions, such as "sit" or "heel."

Give each dog her own leash. Walking two dogs can either double your pleasure or double your trouble. Some professional walkers use leash couplers to link two or more dogs. Manheim recommends using separate leashes, one or more in each hand. And be sure to take up most of the slack, she adds. Giving two dogs too much freedom almost guarantees that there are going to be tangled feet—theirs or yours.

FAST FIX Dogs who are well-trained (or elderly) can enjoy a slow, stately walk. Dogs who are exuberant and seething with energy, however, need to move quickly—not only because it helps them dispel energy but also because it makes it harder for them to get distracted. Walking fast is the best way to keep dogs focused on you rather than on what's happening around them, says Manheim.

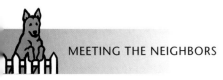
Tied in Knots

There might be a dog who has never gotten tangled in her leash or tripped her owner during an evening walk. But probably not. The length and flexibility that make leashes versatile also make them difficult to control.

Any dog can learn basic leash lessons such as sit or heel in a few weeks. The real challenge comes when you're confronted with real-life problems that aren't always taught in obedience class. Like picking up dog poop when you have a plastic bag in one hand and a squiggling, pulling leash in the other. Or controlling a dog who keeps pulling no matter how much you pull back. Or budging a dog who, for reasons known only to her, simply refuses to move.

None of these situations is difficult to handle—once you know a few tricks.

Cleaning Up Poop

Even Houdini might have found that cleaning up a squishy pile while controlling an eager dog was a serious challenge to his dexterity. People who walk their dogs in public have to deal with this every day. Pet supply stores have some pretty fancy pickup gear, but you don't really need it. The easiest, most efficient way to clean up after your dog also happens to be the cheapest.

Before heading out for your walk, put one or two plastic bags—discarded bread and newspaper wrappers work nicely—in your pocket. When your dog makes a stop, temporarily loop the leash several times around your wrist and put your leash hand inside a plastic bag. Pick up the pile with your bagged hand and use your other hand to turn the bag inside out.

With practice, you can do this in one swift move—it takes about 3 seconds. Twist or knot the top closed and carry it with you until you come to a trash can. People who walk their dogs in city neighborhoods soon have mental maps of the location of every trash can along their usual routes.

Pulling

If dogs went to school, they'd flunk Euclidean geometry. They don't realize—and wouldn't care if they did—that walking in a straight line is the quickest way to get from A to B. Their usual trajectory is a zigzag, usually at a high rate of speed. They know they're on a leash, but they also know that the leash moves when they do—if they pull hard enough.

There are many ways to stop the pulling. Here are a couple that you may want to try.

Don't resist or pull back on the leash when your dog surges forward. Instead, turn your body slightly, plant your feet—and stop. Dogs instinctively pull when something is pulling them, but they tend to give up when they get the feeling that whatever they're attached to isn't going to budge. Plus, stopping abruptly will cause their collars to give a quick snap, a sensation they'd just as soon avoid.

Dogs only strain against their leashes when they're more focused on the world around them than on their owners. To bring your dog's attention back to you, wait until she forges ahead the length of the leash. Then abruptly turn and walk the other way. This move always takes dogs by surprise, and dogs don't like surprises. They soon learn that they're more comfortable when they match their steps with yours.

One way to deal with a pulling dog is to turn your body slightly, plant your feet, and wait. Resume your walk when your dog releases the tension on the leash.

CALL FOR HELP

No one will ever know what they're thinking, but some dogs (usually puppies) get frightened by the oddest things: stairs, lampposts, doorways, even an empty potato chip bag.

Most dogs outgrow their fears, but sometimes they don't—and what began as a little bit of anxiety can turn into a full-fledged phobia. They won't get over it on their own, says Robin Kovary, director of the American Dog Trainers Network in New York City. At soon as you notice signs of unreasonable fears, talk to your veterinarian, who may refer you to a behaviorist. Phobias can be cured, but it's a time-consuming process. In addition, some dogs may need medications such as Prozac (fluoxetine) to help them cope a little more easily.

Abruptly turning and walking the other way when your dog starts pulling will give her an unpleasant surprise. She'll give up and learn that it pays to watch you rather than surging ahead.

Balking

It usually happens when dogs see something that scares them. It could be another dog or a person approaching, or it could be a street sign halfway up the block. Whatever it is, they usually respond by freezing solid or by trying to pull another way. Balky behavior isn't difficult to stop, but you have to work at it. Merely pulling at the leash won't help because dogs who are scared aren't about to cooperate.

When you're approaching whatever it is your dog is afraid of, put yourself in the middle to create a little distance. Happily encourage your dog to hurry past. You'll probably have to lay on the enthusiasm pretty thick, but as long as she has a buffer zone and a lot of praise, she'll probably hurry past. Then praise her some more and give her a treat.

STRANGE behavior

Name FRITZ

Breed GREYHOUND

Age 3

The Behavior

Fritz retired from racing soon after his second birthday, but he didn't retire his love for speed. He launches into round-the-house relays a couple of times a day. He leaps on furniture and takes furious laps around the coffee table. But as his owners soon discovered, there are really two Fritzes: Inside Fritz and Outside Fritz.

Inside Fritz is pure energy, exuberant and full of fun. Outside Fritz doesn't care about speed at all. In fact, he gets so frightened when he's out of the house that he barely lifts a paw. He only trembles, ducks his head, tucks his tail, and tries to hide behind his owners' legs. They understand that the racing life can be a hard one, and it breaks their hearts to see how frightened Fritz becomes.

The Solution

Sadly, most racing dogs are isolated from the world beyond their kennels and the track. They don't meet many people and they don't go for many walks. At an age when other puppies are exploring the world, most of these dogs are cooped up in crates. "Fritz probably received no socialization in the world outside of the track," says Liz Palika, a trainer in Oceanside, California, and author of *All Dogs Need Some Training*. As with many working greyhounds, he may have developed a fear of open places because he was never exposed to them before.

"His owners will have to concentrate on getting him used to the outside world," Palika explains. Because he's so frightened, they'll have to start small—running in the yard and driveway, for example. Once Fritz feels more comfortable when he's outside his own home, they can start thinking about taking him for walks around the block or to a nearby park. It takes time and patience, but most dogs can learn to overcome this type of fear, she says.

In some cases, in fact, they recover a little too well. Greyhounds are bred to run; the urge for speed is part of their very fiber. "Once Fritz does overcome his fear, he should only be allowed to run in secure locations, because running can be so intoxicating for this breed that they sometimes forget where they are and run right away," says Palika.

CHAPTER TWENTY-TWO

MEETING OTHER DOGS

Some dogs go over the top when greeting other dogs. Some are shy and wary.
And others bristle at the very sight of other dogs. Dogs can have greeting rituals that are
very different from people's—but they can all learn to be a little more gracious.

Stan Chappell of Vienna, Virginia, is a pretty tolerant guy. And he likes most dogs. But when it comes to one dog—his brother-in-law's dachshund, Jackson—his tolerance goes out the window.

"I can't stand it when Jackson arrives at our house," Chappell says. "As soon as he comes in, he goes after my dog, Cory. He starts sniffing Cory's rear end and won't stop. That animal is nothing but a sex maniac."

From a human point of view, Chappell's exasperation is understandable. If any of our human friends greeted us by sniffing between our legs, we'd be appalled, to say the least. We have more discreet ways of saying hello. But dogs routinely sniff each other's private areas—and ours, for that matter. From their perspective, it's the right thing to do.

This is just one of many doggy social gestures that are entirely different from those employed by people; and the differences in perception can lead to clashing agendas. Dogs have a right to be themselves and enjoy the company of other dogs. On the other hand, no one wants to shrink with embarrassment every time their dog encounters another dog. Dogs will never stand up on their hind legs and shake hands, but they can learn to be a little more civil.

Who Are You?

Dogs' greeting rituals are just as complex and multifaceted as our own. They use one greeting when they encounter dogs that they know and another when meeting strangers. Appearances notwithstanding, they're remarkably circumspect and polite in the ways they say hi.

Once dogs make eye contact, they begin walking toward each other. Along the way, they probably stop to sniff some grass or clover. This

This beagle and golden retriever are introducing themselves by sniffing each other's faces. Next, they'll move their attention rearward.

is a way of signaling that they're not aggressive. More important, it demonstrates that they're not about to commit the sin of staring, which is a sign of hostility, says John C. Wright, Ph.D., certified applied animal behaviorist, professor of psychology at Mercer University in Macon, Georgia, and author of *The Dog Who Would Be King*. When they're finally close enough, they start to sniff, usually beginning with the head and ears and then moving south.

This Samoyed's relaxed body language shows that he doesn't feel threatened by the stranger's inspection.

There's a good reason that they sniff the nether regions, Dr. Wright explains. The anal and genital areas—and to a lesser extent, the insides of the ears, along the lips, and the top of the head—are packed with glands that release intriguing, informative scents. A quick sniff tells dogs such things as sex, age, and sexual receptiveness.

Jackson the dachshund probably isn't thinking about sex at all when he sniffs Cory's rear end. In all likelihood, he's simply trying to remember who Cory is.

Social Gestures

Dogs' basic greeting rituals are easy to recognize, but the messages they convey are complex. If there are a lot of dogs in your neighborhood, you'll witnesses all of these signals at one time or another. Knowing what dogs are saying is the only way to know whether the encounter you're witnessing is scary or safe. And it's helpful to remember that all of this sniffing, peeing, and leaning has very little to do with you. It's a dog thing, and human notions of manners are really beside the point.

"Don't mess with me." Dogs are intensely conscious of status and power. Even in today's modern, protected world, where status doesn't play a role in survival, they continue to assert their supremacy by barking furiously, staring and swishing their tails, or growling. A dog who displays these and other aggressive signals is telling other dogs to keep their distance. In addition, he may be warning them to stay away from you. "Sometimes, dogs are trying to take responsibility for protecting their owners," Dr. Wright explains.

"Hi, who are you?" In a world of short leashes, it's difficult for dogs to meet other dogs. The only way they can do it is to strain and pull at their leashes. They're not trying to be disrespectful of you, Dr. Wright explains. They're just trying to fulfill their canine obligations.

"Who's the boss?" Since dogs are always concerned about social status, their first order of business is to determine which, if either, dog deserves special respect. There's no avoiding this. All dogs think about leadership. This was a critical concern in the days before dogs decided to cast their lots with people, and the issue is bound to surface whenever two or more dogs meet.

What usually happens is that one dog stands stone-still while the other, more forward dog stands next to and over him. The dog who is dominant may follow this towering move by darting his nose up and down his fellow's spine, as though he were a bird pecking seeds. Assuming that the "lower" dog isn't interested in proclaiming his own high status, it's usually at this point that he rolls over on his back—and possibly urinates all over the sidewalk.

"Yup, I'm the boss." It's a very aggressive move, but dogs do it all the time. Right after they meet and dispense with the sniffing preliminaries, one dog may urinate very near the other one. It's his way of proclaiming that he's the boss of the pair, says Sarah Wilson, a trainer in Gardiner, New York, and co-author of *Childproofing Your Dog*. There's a good chance that the second dog will acquiesce. Or he'll express his disagreement by urinating on top of the first dog's puddle. At this point, there's no predicting what will happen next—it's up to dog number one to decide if he wants to challenge the statement laid down by dog number two. Chances are good, however, that the dogs will dispense with all of this social posturing and simply start to have a good time.

"I want to play." Dogs have an unmistakable way of signaling that they're in the mood for fun. It's called a play bow, and the name describes precisely what they do—lower their front legs close to the ground while stick-

ing their bottoms way up in the air. This posture is usually accompanied by a swiftly wagging tail and a nearly human-looking grin. It means that a dog is in high spirits and is inviting the other dog—or person—to hurry up and play.

"I'm going to win if we fight." Dogs have powerful bodies and equally powerful jaws, but they still prefer posturing to fighting. Conflicts in the wild are costly, and dogs have wisely learned that a good bluff can work just as well as a direct attack and is a heck of a lot safer. But sometimes, they do take that final step. What you're likely to see is one or both dogs rising up on his rear legs and cuffing and grappling with his front paws. It's very similar to the position dogs use when play-fighting, and it's not always easy to tell the difference—except that true aggression is invariably accompanied by snarling and growling. "You'll know in about 5 seconds whether it's going to be a fight or playtime," says Dr. Wright.

The play-bow—a gesture in which dogs stick their rears in the air and wag their tails—is how they invite people and other dogs to join in a game.

143

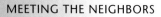

This Border collie is blowing off energy before he goes near other dogs. It's probably the best way to keep him calm.

Peaceful Promenades

You don't have to be fluent in dog to know when basic good manners are being breached. In a way, this has very little to do with canine etiquette and a lot to do with human expectations. It may be natural for dogs to snarl and lunge to establish dominance, for example, but you're not going to win many friends when it's your dog doing the lunging. Dogs will never give up their natural, if somewhat gamey, rituals. But they can adjust their styles to suit the people in their lives. The people, in turn, have to get used to the idea that dogs are going to do some pretty unpleasant things—if not sniffing, then urinating, and if not urinating, then humping. They've been doing them for thousands of years, and they don't need a lot of help from us.

Take the edge off their energy. Most dogs spend a lot of time lying around and not doing much. But there's a volcano of energy under the surface. Like children let out of school on a summer day, they nearly come unhinged with excitement when they get a chance to play and interact. The more their energy is seething, the more likely they are to go overboard with greetings—which means you'll see a lot of bottom-sniffing, humping, leaning, and licking.

Giving dogs lots of exercise can take the edge off their over-the-top excitement, according to Carol Lea Benjamin, a trainer and author of *Dog Problems*. In fact, people who regularly take their dogs out in public often make sure that the first half of the walk is in a relatively dog-free environment. This allows their dogs to blow off steam before they meet other dogs along the way.

Step in and take charge. It would be presumptuous to instruct an Italian on the proper pronunciation of "ciao." Similarly, dogs know their own social rules better than we ever will, which is why it's usually best to step back and let them do what they do. This advice changes, however, when there's aggression in the air.

It's easy to stop problems when both dogs are on leashes. All their people have to do is pull them in different directions. When your dog is on a leash and the other dog isn't, however, you'll have to assert your moral authority indirectly. "Look at the other dog and say, 'Stop' or 'Go away' in a very firm, loud voice," says Kathy McCoubrey, a trainer in Broad Run, Virginia. "This can break the concentration of the other dog so that he'll stop in his tracks. I've tried this myself and found it very effective, even though I'm not a physically imposing person."

Let them choose their friends. All dogs may look more or less alike to us, but they have their own criteria for friendship that have to be

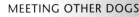

respected, says Sandy Myers, owner of Narnia Pet Behavior and Training in Naperville, Illinois. "We can't pick our children's friends, even though we try; and we can't pick our dogs' friends, either," she says. She recommends watching the body language of both dogs when they meet. As long as you see play signals—a loosely wagging tail, a happy grin, and eager sprinting back and forth—you'll know they're getting along.

Tense body language doesn't mean dogs are going to fight, she adds. Many dogs are nervous about meeting other dogs, and they'll naturally be a little stiff. But you still don't want to bring dogs together if the signs aren't right, especially when they're on leashes. Dogs who are running free can approach or run away if they want to. When they're both on leashes, they may feel trapped—and that will make them even more tense and anxious. "I generally cross to the other side of the street when I see that we're approaching an unfamiliar person or dog, and most other dog owners in my subdivision do the same," says Dr. Wright. "Later, if we keep seeing each other, my dog becomes more receptive, and introductions generally go fine."

Walk quickly—in the other direction. Some dogs always have something to prove. If your dog has a chip on his shoulder—or there's another dog in the neighborhood who does—even casual sniff-and-greets can quickly get ugly. Even if the dogs don't get close enough to squabble, you may find yourself struggling to pull the leash one way while your dog is struggling to go the other.

When peace isn't possible, retreat is the only sensible option. Immediately turn and walk the other way when you think there may be an unpleasant confrontation, Dr. Wright recommends. Even dogs who dislike each other on sight can't do much when they're on opposite sides of the street.

Keep your voice down. When dogs do fight, it's natural for their people to shout and yell. It doesn't help, says Dr. Wright. If anything, it increases the level of tension. A better approach is to keep your voice low and employ diversionary tactics, such as moving quickly in the opposite direction.

POOCH PUZZLER

Do dogs have stinky feet?

Despite their reputations for having doggy breath and wet-dog odors, most dogs actually smell pretty good—assuming, of course, that they haven't been rolling in dung or raiding the cat box lately.

But there is one area where dogs smell just as musty as people, and that's on the bottoms of their feet, says John C. Wright, Ph.D., certified applied animal behaviorist, professor of psychology at Mercer University in Macon, Georgia, and author of *The Dog Who Would Be King*. "There are pores in a dog's foot pads through which odor-bearing moisture comes out," says Dr. Wright. "This means a dog can sniff where another dog has walked and know that the first dog has been there."

The odors can be quite strong—but only to dogs. People aren't really aware of the odors, says Dr. Wright. Even if dogs did have a sour-sock smell, they wouldn't want it washed away, because they need the odors to communicate with other dogs.

STOPPING A DOGFIGHT

Most dogfights are nasty, brutish, and short. They rarely last more than a few seconds, but that's more than enough for the dogs to inflict serious injuries. It's up to the humans to break up fights—without getting hurt themselves.

"When your dog is fighting, he probably is not going to be able to recognize you as his loving owner," says Steve Aiken, an animal behaviorist in Wichita, Kansas. "He may be a very sweet licking machine at home, but in the middle of a dogfight, he's acting on tens of thousands of years of instinct. If you get in the middle, expect to get bitten."

There are several ways to stop or at least interrupt a fight. Here are a few strategies that trainers recommend.

Soak them with water. Dogs hate getting splashed, and sometimes spraying the combatants with water from a hose will break them up. It doesn't always work, but for dogs who are too big to separate physically, it may be your only choice.

Put down a barrier. When small dogs are fighting, throw a blanket or even your coat over both dogs. This will protect you from bites and scratches as you physically separate them.

CHAPTER TWENTY-THREE

MEETING CATS

Cats often prefer privacy, but dogs see everything that
moves as a potential plaything. Because of these conflicting agendas,
dogs and cats need a little help working things out.

Cats are small, they zigzag, and they have interesting smells. They're about the best fuzzy play toys a dog could ask for. Cats, of course, have a different perspective, which is why worlds collide when cats and dogs come face-to-face.

Cats get pretty tired of being harassed by man's best friend, and people get pretty tired of rescuing cats who have been scared up trees, or being dragged across the street every time their dogs take off in pursuit.

Teaching dogs to be more considerate of cats is a challenge because every fiber in their bodies wants to give chase. Dogs as well as cats are nat-

ural predators whose instincts tell them to chase whatever moves—especially things that are smaller than they are, says Debra Forthman, Ph.D., director of field conservation at Zoo Atlanta in Georgia. The more cats run, the more dogs want to chase them, she explains.

Meeting the Neighbors

Dogs and cats aren't natural enemies, but they are very different. Dogs tend to be social, extroverted, and physical, while cats are more solitary and diffident. "A dog looks at a cat and says, 'Wow! Here's something to play with!'" says Lewis Cooper, D.V.M., a veterinarian in Rockville, Maryland. "The cat just says, 'Get away from me.'"

Cats will never learn to be more like dogs, but dogs can learn to be more catlike—or at least more polite—in their greetings. It's easiest to teach young dogs to respect cats, but even dogs who are set in their ways can learn additional social graces.

Introduce them slowly.
Dogs rarely chase cats whom they live with, because they understand that these little creatures are their friends and deserve a

BREED SPECIFIC

Most dogs chase cats for a quick thrill, but for some breeds it's more like business. Dogs bred for guarding, such as pit bulls and Rottweilers, and those bred for hunting small game, such as beagles and Jack Russell terriers (right), may have a hard time resisting the chase.

little respect. You can help them form the same feelings for cats in the neighborhood by making the proper introductions.

"You have to allow them to develop affection for each other, and that means introducing them several times for short periods each time," says Dr. Cooper. When you're out on walks and your dog is on a leash, let him approach cats, but hold him back so he approaches slowly, Dr. Cooper advises. Many cats will welcome this type of controlled interaction and will come up and give a sniff. As often as you can, make additional overtures—to the same cat and to any others you happen to meet—letting your dog get a little closer each time. He'll start to under-

stand that every cat is an individual to be respected, rather than potential prey to be chased.

Show by example. Dogs look to their humans for guidance in how to act in different situations. Dr. Cooper recommends crouching down between your dog and the cat he's meeting. Hold your dog with one hand and pet the cat with the other. "Your dog will begin to see the relationship between you and the cat," he says. After that, he'll want to follow your lead, Dr. Cooper explains.

Watch for signs of tension. Most dogs get along fine with cats, but others will bristle at the very idea. So keep an eye on your dog and back off if he shows signs of aggression, says Mary Beth Dearing, D.V.M., a veterinarian in Alexandria, Virginia.

All under One Roof

It doesn't take a lot of diplomacy for dogs to get along with—or at least ignore—cats on the other side of the street. When they meet cats on their own turf, however, things get a little more complicated. Even though they'll probably learn to get along with a feline who is just joining the family, the first few weeks may be tense. Here's what experts recommend that you do to keep your dog on his best behavior and ensure that the fur doesn't start flying.

Keep them apart—but together. Dogs are very territorial and don't always take kindly to newcomers, whether they're cats or other dogs. Unless you give them time to adjust, they may react in less than positive ways. Dr. Forthman recommends putting up a baby gate with

When people make it clear that cats are welcome members of the family, it doesn't take dogs long to accept the newcomers.

Dogs and cats aren't natural enemies. In fact, they'll often become the best of friends, especially when their owners encourage them to get along.

your dog on one side and the cat on the other. This allows them to see and smell each other for a few days. When your cat is approaching the gate without fear and your dog seems more curious than excited, you can take down the gate and let them mingle, she says.

Let them work it out. People always want to get involved when their pets are bickering, but this usually makes things worse, says Vivian Jamieson, D.V.M., a veterinary ophthalmologist in Mount Pleasant, South Carolina. Dogs and cats need to establish a natural hierarchy in which one pet has lower status relative to the other, she explains. People who step in and scold the one who is more dominant are merely prolonging the struggle. "If you constantly support the submissive one, you're going to encourage more fighting," she says.

Provide for quick escapes. Even in the happiest households, a dog's sense of fun may include such things as nipping, wrestling, or even shaking a cat in his mouth—behavior that's sure to elicit a hiss-and-swat reaction or at least a few moments of panic. Cats always need

a way to escape, says Dr. Forthman. Some people install a cat door that's too small to admit a dog. Others put up a cat tree that allows cats to get high and out of reach in a hurry. Cats who know they can escape whenever they want are much more likely to accept a dog's idea of fun without launching a full-fledged attack.

 FAST FIX No matter how much dogs enjoy chasing cats, they usually enjoy food even more. Some veterinarians recommend keeping treats in your pocket for a few days after bringing a new pet into the family. When your dog starts his boisterous behavior, flip him a treat. Dogs can't eat and chase at the same time, and given the choice, they usually opt to eat.

POOCH ?? PUZZLER

Why do dogs love cat food?

Given a choice between eating dog kibble or cat food, dogs will invariably turn their backs on their own food and clean out the cat's bowl instead. Dogs are naturally competitive when it comes to food, and undoubtedly they enjoy the feeling of "winning" the extra serving. But the main reason that they crave cat chow is that it tastes very good. Cats need more fat in their diets than dogs, so their food is filled with fat flavors. In addition, cats won't eat food unless it has a strong taste and even stronger aroma, says Lewis Cooper, D.V.M., a veterinarian in Rockville, Maryland. The same smells and tastes that cats find so attractive act like magnets for dogs, he explains.

CHAPTER TWENTY-FOUR

MEETING STRANGERS

If we spent as much time alone as dogs do, we'd get pretty excited—or nervous, shy, or ecstatic—about meeting people, too. But every dog, whether she gets out every day or once a week, can learn to greet people politely and with polish.

Human greetings must seem strange and standoffish to dogs. We greet strangers with nods of the head and polite handshakes. Dogs are much less reserved. Their tendency is to meet people with all the subtlety of laser-guided missiles: barking with pleasure when people approach, running in excited circles, jumping up for paw-to-chest encounters. Their natural instinct is to be very physical when meeting someone.

In addition, the human world, from their point of view, is a confusing swirl of moving legs and arms, and a babble of words that they don't understand. It's as though every day were a day in Disneyland: Their senses can get overly stimulated, and meeting new people ratchets up the excitement even more. Things that we take for granted—the jangle of keys, the rustle of a parka, the scent of perfume—make them think that wonderful

Dogs who have met a lot of people from a young age learn to take the experience for granted.

things are happening, and they can barely contain themselves.

Some dogs are better social emissaries than others, of course. Those who regularly meet strangers get fairly blasé about the whole thing, while those who rarely meet people tend to go over the top, says Quenten London, a training consultant with the National Institute of Dog Training in Los Angeles, who recommends introducing dogs to as many people as possible while they're still young and impressionable.

Restoring Civility

Americans who travel overseas are often mystified by the social expectations in the different cultures that they visit. Bowing, touching forearms, and kissing are just a few of the socially correct ways that strangers greet each other. The confusion is even greater for dogs here at home. Their every instinct tells them to greet people dog-style. They want to use their mouths, paws, and some-

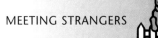

times their entire bodies to communicate greetings. If they aren't taught not to do these things—and given other, more polite alternatives—their social standing among the neighbors isn't likely to thrive.

Dogs do have one great advantage over people: They're very eager to do the right thing. Even without formal obedience lessons, most dogs can learn the rudiments of human greetings fairly quickly. Here's what experts advise.

Give them time to adjust. It's not an accident that you and your dog will usually spend a few minutes alone before the veterinarian comes into the examining room. Giving dogs a few minutes to explore their surroundings helps them get over the excitement of being someplace new and meeting new people, says Lewis Cooper, D.V.M., a veterinarian in Rockville, Maryland. This makes it easier for veterinarians to look them over and do their jobs, he explains.

You can use a similar technique when you and your dog are out in public. Suppose you're going around the block, where you'll certainly encounter people you haven't seen before. Before setting out, give your dog a chance to get used to being outside. Let her sniff around the

Giving dogs a chance to nose around a bit before going for walks allows them to calm down before meeting others.

front yard for a few minutes. Encourage her to dawdle by the telephone pole on the corner and the fire hydrant around the block. Dogs who have time to absorb the newness of their environments are able to dispel surplus energy and get used to the sights and sounds. This helps them be a little calmer when the environment also includes new people.

Give a silent lesson. Dogs crave our attention and approval, which is why punishment often isn't necessary—just letting them know you don't approve of something is often enough to make them stop. Suppose your dog greets people by jumping up. Pointedly ignoring the

BREED SPECIFIC

Dogs' love for people knows no breed boundaries, but sporting dogs, such as retrievers, setters, pointers, and spaniels, are among the most even-tempered and friendly because they've been bred to work very closely with people.

151

Why do dogs mount people's legs?

Even dogs who are slow to warm up to people sometimes greet them in the most intimate and inappropriate way of all—by firmly wrapping themselves around the nearest leg and eagerly humping away.

Veterinarians call this mounting behavior, and it's extremely common, especially in dogs who haven't been neutered. It's mainly a guy thing, but some females do it, too. It looks sexual, but that's not what it's about, says Jeanne Saddler, a trainer and the owner of Myriad Dog Training in Manhattan, Kansas. It's really about getting ahead in the world.

As with other forms of physical contact, such as jumping up and putting their paws on other dogs' shoulders, dogs mount each other when they want to signal that they're dominant and have greater social status. In the wild, dogs who were dominant ate better than other dogs and had more offspring. It was a good message to send.

Dogs can certainly tell the difference between a person's leg and another dog, but the message is more or less the same: "I'm the one in charge around here, and I'm doing this to make sure you know it, too."

Stand on the leash. It's asking a lot to expect people you don't know to stand still while getting bowled over by 85 pounds of canine excitement. You may need to take more of an active approach. Trainers recommend using the leash to curtail inappropriate greetings. Actually, you don't have to do much of anything. When your dog approaches a stranger with her usual lack of decorum, quickly step on the slack portion of the leash. Whether your dog is going in for a sniff or a full-fledged jump, taking up the slack will bring her to an abrupt halt, says Jeanne Saddler, a trainer and the owner of Myriad Dog Training in Manhattan, Kansas. "This way, no one is the bad guy," she explains. "The only jerking is what the dog did to herself."

Wrap it around your waist. Every dog can learn to greet strangers politely, but it won't happen right away. In the meantime, trainers sometimes recommend wrapping the leash loosely around your waist when

Wrapping the leash around your waist makes it easier to control a dog who is intent on giving an overly exuberant greeting.

behavior—and, more important, encouraging others to ignore it—takes away the satisfaction. Some dogs will simply give it up, says Nicholas Dodman, professor of behavioral pharmacology and director of the Animal Behavior Clinic at Tufts University School of Veterinary Medicine in North Grafton, Massachusetts, and author of *Dogs Behaving Badly.*

people are approaching. This helps in two ways: First, it shortens the leash, giving the dog less room to sniff and lunge. Second, it also allows you to pull your dog back just by swiveling your hips. Putting the brakes on her forward momentum works better than giving a prolonged pull, if only because dogs tend to respond to pulls with pulls of their own. A quick jerk is a message they can't ignore. They don't forget it, either, and they learn that moving quickly toward strangers invariably gets them pulled back.

FAST FIX Dogs learn quickest when their lessons are linked to food. Suppose your dog always lunges forward when people approach. After stopping her forward momentum—by putting your foot on the leash, for example—and waiting a moment for her to calm down, give her a biscuit or some other treat. She'll associate the food with the emotion of the moment, which will be calmness and not excitement, Saddler says. "Before long, your dog will teach herself the lesson she needed to learn," she explains.

It's a Scary World

The vast majority of dogs love people and are excited—maybe too excited—to meet them. But some dogs are simply afraid. They're afraid of people they don't know. They're afraid of people with loud voices or tall people or young people who run around a lot. Sometimes, they're afraid because of something unpleasant that happened

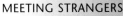

CALL FOR HELP

It's natural for dogs to bark, bristle, or growl when strangers approach their territory. At home, this protective urge helps people feel safe, and it's not entirely a bad thing. When it occurs in public, however, it makes other people nervous—and for good reason. Even small dogs can give very strong bites, which is why aggressive behavior is so scary.

Dogs who act aggressively toward the people around them have forgotten the first and most important part of their covenant: "In exchange for food, love, and a warm place to sleep, we will always remember that you, not we, are the ones in charge."

Aggressive behavior isn't that hard to stop, although you'll probably need help from an expert. It's worth doing right away because dogs who act aggressively invariably get worse unless they're stopped immediately, says Nicholas Dodman, professor of behavioral pharmacology and director of the Animal Behavior Clinic at Tufts University School of Veterinary Medicine in North Grafton, Massachusetts, and author of *Dogs Behaving Badly*.

While your dog is learning new rules, try to avoid making too much eye contact, Dodman adds. Dogs instinctively view direct eye contact as a challenge. Even though most dogs learn to accept eye contact as a perfectly normal human thing, those who tend to be aggressive may not tolerate it at all. So make eye contact only briefly, or, better yet, avoid it entirely until your dog is doing the things she's supposed to do.

before. And sometimes that's just how they are. Dogs who are shy or naturally nervous or who have never been around people very much tend to shy away—or, conversely, to growl or get aggressive—when people come too close. And for these dogs, across the street may feel a little too close.

Except for dogs whose fears run deep, it's usually easy to help them relax around people. As with so many other lessons, it's easiest to teach dogs to be calm and friendly when you pamper their tummies. That's why Saddler developed a special training exercise that she calls the cookie technique. The idea is pretty simple. By teaching dogs to associate a word with their favorite foods, it's possible to actually change their moods just by saying the word. Here's how it works.

1. Give your dog a treat several times a day while saying "cookie." It's not easy for dogs to learn human words, but they have no trouble at all remembering words that indicate that food is about to arrive. Keep doing this for several weeks until your dog gets in a tail-wagging mood whenever she hears the word "cookie."

2. Whenever you take your dog where people are—or when people come to the house—fill your pockets with cookies. "The instant your dog sees a stranger, before she has decided whether

At Your Service

Delta is a little dog who does a big job with amazing grace. The 9-year-old papillon throws every ounce of his 6 pounds (he's a little less than a foot tall) into helping his owner, Lauren Wilson, maintain her mobility and independence. Wilson, who is disabled, has come to count on Delta, an exceptional example of the discipline and abilities of service dogs—pups who are trained to help people with disabilities.

Working together, Wilson and Delta are a strong team. "He's my helper and he's family," says Wilson, of Silver Spring, Maryland. "I use multiple commands to get him to jump on kitchen counters and slide cans and other objects to me, push the proper buttons on the microwave, or even climb into the clothes dryer to retrieve clothes from the back that are beyond my reach." On grocery day, other shoppers watch in amazement as Wilson points out foods from her motorized chair and Delta leaps onto the shelves to deliver the goods.

Few dogs beat Delta when it comes to dedication, intelligence, and a sense of humor. Once, Delta had to spend some time at the veterinarian's. "I asked the vet's assistant not to crate him," Wilson says, "because he would do anything to get back to me." The assistant decided to tuck Delta into a crate anyway. A few moments later, to everyone's surprise, Delta emerged on his own from the vet's back office, followed by a few new friends. "He had not only opened his own door to get back to me," Wilson says, "he had let all the other animals out, as well."

or not she's going to be scared, say 'Do you think he has a cookie?'" When she looks happy at the mention of her favorite word, give her a treat. If you do this all the time, she'll discover that meeting new people always seems to coincide with her favorite activity of all. And it's very hard for dogs to be frightened at the same time that they're thinking about food.

154

STRANGE behavior

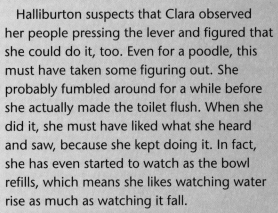

Name CLARA

Breed STANDARD POODLE

Age 2

The Behavior

Clara drinks out of the toilet. That's not too surprising, because most dogs find that the toilet bowl is a convenient place to get a drink. But Clara doesn't stop with a little liquid refreshment. When she's done drinking, she raises her paw and jiggles the handle until the toilet flushes. She stands and watches as the water goes down. Then she walks out of the bathroom. Her owners don't mind that Clara is wasting water. But they're getting a little unnerved—not only because they hear the toilet flushing when they're the only people home but also because it seems crazy that Clara is able to do it at all.

The Solution

Making the mental connection between the toilet handle and the resulting flush is quite an accomplishment. Among dogs, it's nearly the equivalent of discovering quantum physics. It makes sense that a poodle made the great discovery because these dogs are exceptionally bright, says Judith Halliburton, a trainer and behaviorist in Albuquerque, New Mexico, and author of *Raising Rover*.

Halliburton suspects that Clara observed her people pressing the lever and figured that she could do it, too. Even for a poodle, this must have taken some figuring out. She probably fumbled around for a while before she actually made the toilet flush. When she did it, she must have liked what she heard and saw, because she kept doing it. In fact, she has even started to watch as the bowl refills, which means she likes watching water rise as much as watching it fall.

There's another explanation, as well. Most dogs drink their water out of large bowls. The water may get changed every day, but it still gets warm and stale-tasting. It's possible that Clara flushes the toilet to get a drink of fresh, flowing water. Watching the action is just part of the fun.

If Clara's owners truly dislike her newfound bathroom habit, they could stop it just by closing the bathroom door, Halliburton says. Even closing the lid may work because that would take away the visual thrill. Of course, it's always possible that Clara would discover how to raise the lid, in which case they would have to try something else.

CHAPTER TWENTY-FIVE

PLANNING PIT STOPS

Nature's call doesn't always come at convenient times. It sounds in the middle of
the night or on busy sidewalks or on the neighbor's lawn. You can't ignore the call,
but you can work with dogs to ensure that it comes at better times.

Dogs aren't known for their delicate manners or their sense of discretion, as Jennifer Hannum, a university student in Philadelphia, can attest. Every day, she walks her 10-year-old Labrador mix to a pleasant park two blocks from her home; and every day, she has to wait, an embarrassed look on her face, while her dog takes a bathroom break in the middle of the street or in front of the one house where the occupants happen to be outside.

"It doesn't matter if she's been inside for 30 minutes or 8 hours," Hannum says. "She always stops on the spur of the moment, and it's never where I want to stop."

Social Rules, Physical Limits

People with large enclosed yards don't have to worry about their dogs' bathroom habits because their entire lawns make great commodes. Those who live in apartments or big cities, however, often take their dogs for three or four walks a day. Even short walks become an adventure when:

- Dogs insist on watering every vertical object or speck of dirt on the sidewalk.
- They take their bathroom breaks at lousy times, like when you're crossing the street or standing in front of an outdoor cafe.

- They refuse to go at all. This usually happens during rainstorms or at 3:00 A.M., while their owners impatiently wait for them to get with the program.

"Dogs aren't under the same social rules that we are," says Brian Kilcommons, a trainer and behavioral expert in Gardiner, New York, and co-author of *Good Owners, Great Dogs.* "You have to understand that dogs relieve themselves at inappropriate moments, and that dogs have limitations."

One of those limitations, of course, is access. Except for dogs with doggy doors, they only go outside when people take them out. That often means going 10 to 12 hours without a break, and that's stretching the limits of their holding capacity, says Mike Richards, D.V.M., a veterinarian in Cobbs Creek, Virginia.

There's also the social aspect of bathroom breaks. People go for relief, but dogs have more in mind because they use urine as a way of communicating with other dogs, says Kimberly Barry, Ph.D., a certified applied animal behaviorist in Austin, Texas. They prefer to stop in places where other dogs have stopped—at light poles, in neighbors' front yards, or in the middle of the street. And of course, dogs don't have the same social inhibitions that people do. Leaving a pile on a busy sidewalk is no more embarrassing for them than stopping to sniff a chrysanthemum. Why wait to get to the park when this nice patch of sidewalk is right here?

Planned Convenience

Any dog, even one who hasn't had a lot of formal education, can learn to make his pit stops at times and places that are a little more convenient for you, Kilcommons says.

Keep to a schedule. Dogs have a hazy sense of time, but their internal clocks are as accurate as a Swiss watch. If you take them out at the same times every day—especially after they eat, when everything in their bodies is churning—they will learn to anticipate these breaks and will be less desperate when you walk out the door.

Teach a potty prompt. Just as dogs can easily learn to sit or lie down, they can also learn to do their business when you ask them to. The trick is to practice the commands when they're ready to do what comes naturally. When your dog is squatting or lifting a leg, give a command such as "go now." When he goes—as he surely will—praise the heck out of him, Kilcommons says. If you do this several times a day for a few weeks, your dog will begin to link the words with the action. And once he understands what you're saying, he'll look forward to doing it— and getting the nice praise that follows.

Watch their body language. Even dogs who know what they're supposed to do aren't always able to do it—either because they waited too long before going outside or because their owners weren't paying attention. To help your dog understand that he should always wait for

This Australian shepherd is glad to take his breaks on command, although having a nice tree nearby is always a treat.

the "go" command, you have to watch his body language to see when he's getting restless or uncomfortable. When you see that, quickly take him where you want him to go and give the command. The more you practice together and the fewer accidents there are, the easier it will be for him to time his breaks in ways that are most convenient for you.

FAST FIX Dogs aren't always able to go in a hurry just because their owners want them to. "Take a deep breath and run around the block with him," Kilcommons suggests. Exercise speeds the body's metabolism, and most dogs will be ready to take a break within a few minutes.

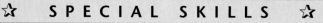

☆ SPECIAL SKILLS ☆

SHAKE HANDS

Shaking hands is always a neighborly thing to do. People do it all the time, and most dogs can learn it, too. For big dogs, especially, an offer to shake hands lets people know that they're friendly as well as socially adept.

1 Ask your dog to sit in front of you. Hold a treat where he can see it, then close your hand so it's out of sight.

2 Put your hand, still closed, just underneath his chin and wait a bit. Eventually, he'll start pawing your hand to get at the treat. As soon as he lifts his paw, praise him and give him the treat. Keep practicing until he starts pawing at your hand as soon as you move it toward his chin. When that happens, start telling him, "Shake hands" when you move your hand forward. Pretty soon, he'll recognize that a proffered hand is always an offer to shake.

SAY HELLO

Any dog can run up to strangers and poke his nose in private places, but only well-behaved dogs can make visitors feel welcome by actually saying hello—or at least giving a well-mannered bark of greeting.

1 Do whatever it takes to make your dog bark. For some dogs, this will mean having someone call at a certain time, or ringing the doorbell. For others, jumping up and down and acting excited will set them off. As soon as your dog barks, tell him, "Say hello."

2 After the first or second bark, give him the treat. Dogs can't eat and bark at the same time, so he'll quiet down right away. When he does, tell him, "Enough." Keep practicing until your dog barks and stops barking with each command. Then take him around to meet the neighbors.

159

GO TO YOUR PLACE

Friendly dogs are nice to be around, but sometimes they get a little too friendly—following you around, nudging you to play, and generally getting underfoot. That's why every dog should have a place of his own, such as a blanket in a corner, where he'll retire when you tell him to.

1 Hold a treat in front of your dog and use it to lure him to "his" place. Encourage him to lie down. When he starts going down, point to the place and say, "Down. Place." Once he's down, give him the treat.

2 Keep practicing until he has the idea. (As he gets more adept, you can quit saying, "Down," and just say, "Place.") Then, start giving the command from farther away. At first, you'll probably be just 1 to 2 feet away. After awhile, you'll be able to point to the place from across the room and he'll quickly go and lie down.

GET YOUR TOY

Experienced hosts put guests at ease by suggesting something enjoyable that they can do together. Dogs can be good hosts, too, by bringing a toy for guests to play with. It's best to practice this trick inside to ensure that your dog doesn't grab his toy and run off behind the rhododendrons.

1 Toss your dog's favorite toy so it lands a few feet away from him. Tell him, "Get your toy," and encourage him to pick it up. When he picks up the toy, have him bring it to you. Praise him lavishly when he does, then give him a treat. After that, encourage him to play with the toy for a moment.

2 Keep practicing until he keeps bringing you the toy, no matter how far away you're standing. After awhile, he'll be more than willing to retrieve the toy from his basket, as well. To entertain guests, you can sit next to them while giving the command. Or ask them to tell your dog, "Get your toy."

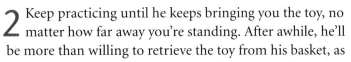

Credits and Acknowledgments

(t=top, b=bottom, l=left, r=right, c=center, F=front, C=cover, B=back)

All photographs are copyright to the sources listed below.

PHOTOGRAPH CREDITS

Ad-Libitum: Stuart Bowey, ic, vib, 2b, 4b, 6t, 7b, 8b, 10t, 11b, 12b, 13t, 14t, 15b, 16b, 17t, 20b, 21t, 23t, 23b, 27t, 28b, 29t, 31t, 32b, 34b, 35b, 36b, 37t, 38b, 39b, 40t, 42b, 44t, 45b, 48b, 49t, 50t, 51b, 52t, 53b, 54b, 55b, 56b, 57b, 58t, 59b, 60b, 63b, 65t, 68t, 69c, 70b, 72b, 73t, 74b, 75b, 76t, 77b, 78t, 79b, 80t, 81t, 88, 91t, 93t, 93b, 94t, 95b, 97t, 99b, 100t, 103t, 104b, 105t, 107t, 109b, 117b, 118b, 119t, 121b, 130b, 131t, 132t, 133b, 134t, 134b, 135t, 136b, 139t, 139b, 135t, 136t, 139b, 140t, 141b, 142t, 143b, 144t, 147b, 149t, 150b, 151t, 152b, 155t, 157t, BCtr, BCbr, BCbl.

Auscape International: Jean-Michel Labat, 98t; Yves Lanceau, 123t; Klein/Hubert-Bios, 136b

Australian Picture Library: John Carnemolla, 25b

Bill Bachman: viiib, 22t, 80b

Norvia Behling: 5b, 46, 66c, BClc

Bruce Coleman Limited: Jane Burton, x, 90b, BCtl

Kent and Donna Dannen: 26b, 120b

Ron Levy: 115t

Ron Kimball: FC

André Martin: 113b

The Photo Library: David Madison, 18

Dale C. Spartas: iic, 25t, 128

Judith E. Strom: 108c, 111t

ILLUSTRATIONS

All illustrations by Chris Wilson/Merilake; icons by Matt Graif

The publisher would like to thank the following people for their assistance in the preparation of this book:

Trudie Craig; Karen Francis at Pawprint; Annabel Fraser; Tracey Jackson.

Special thanks to the following people who kindly brought their dogs to photo shoots:

Kerry Achurch and "Jak"; Lindy Archer and Sue Deehan and "Champagne" and "George"; Tim and Andrea Barnard and "Sam" and "Tessa"; Helen Bateman and "Bonnie"; Esther Blank and "Max"; Corinne and Don Braye and "Minne"; Jenny Bruce and "Stella"; Penny Cass and "Wilma"; Jo Cocks and "Gypsy"; Lindy Coote and "Boo"; Frances Farac and "Madison"; Judith Fox and "Rawson"; Gwynneth Grant and "Max"; Lindy Haynes and "Hudson," "Nelson," and "Panda"; Dinah Holden and "Molly"; Anne Holmes and "Marli"; Ann Howard and "Bella"; Lubasha Macdonald and "Tigra"; Paul McGreevy and "Wally"; Andrew McIntyre and "Abby" and "Daisy"; Rosemary Marin-Guzman and "Biggles"; John Maroulis and "Harry" and "Monty"; John and Hilary Mulquin and "Cleo"; Judith Neilson and "Pepa"; Dan Penny and "Molly"; Jackie Richards and Nick Wiles and "Skipper"; Matthew Robinson and "Jesse"; Denise Rowntree and "Bootsie"; Craig and Melissa Turner and "Carne" and "Flash"; Jan Watson and "Flash" and "Jessie"; Russ Weakley and "Max," "Bob," and "Harry"; Kathryn Weidemier and "Jessika".

Index

Underscored page references indicate sidebars. **Boldface** references indicate illustrations.